W9-BQY-195

INTERACTIVE
PREACHING

INTERACTIVE PREACHING

D. Stephenson Bond

CPB Press
St. Louis, Missouri

© Copyright 1991 CBP Press

All rights reserved. No part of this book may be reproduced without written permission from CBP Press, Box 179, St. Louis, MO 63166.

Scripture quotations not otherwise designated are from the New Revised Standard Version Bible, copyright 1989, Division of Christian Education of the National Council of the Churches of Christ in the United States of America and are used by permission.

Library of Congress Cataloging-in-Publication Data

Bond, D. Stephenson.
    Interactive preaching / by D. Stephenson Bond.
1. Preaching.   2. Public worship.   3. Dialogue sermons.
I. Title.
BV4211.2B63   1991   251   90-20412
ISBN 0-8272-1610-6

Printed in the United States of America

To Heather, with thanks and love.

ACKNOWLEDGMENTS

Many persons played a role in bringing this book and my own interactive preaching to fruition. My deepest gratitude is extended to Gary Smith for the long hours of conversation and his encouragement to venture out of the pulpit as he had broken the ground ahead of me; and to Laura Smith for inspiration, love, and some of the central metaphors of my life. Thank you both for everything.

My sincere appreciation to the people of Garden City Christian Church (Disciples of Christ) in Indianapolis without whom interactive preaching would not have been possible. Thank you for your courage in speaking up and for the many moments recorded in this book. Thank you for tolerating my creativity and encouraging me to reach farther.

Special thanks to David Polk at CBP Press for believing in this book and for the work in bringing it all together.

And finally, my appreciation to Heather, David, and Molly for their patience and the gift of time away from their lives which this book represents.

85036

CONTENTS

PREFACE

I am concerned about the widening gulf between faith and experience—more specifically, about the discrepancy between faith language (the way people, especially ministers, talk about God, church, soul, etc.) and the reference of that language to lived human experience. I am concerned about what I perceive as the poverty of meaning in modern life that results from the failure to ground the imagination of faith in the particular, subjective story of an individual life. I believe that's where a felt sense of meaning comes from: the play of imagination in religious images, woven with the strands of our personal history like a fine tapestry. I am concerned that the tapestry of eternal images is too often hidden from consciousness, and that people are walking around with strands stuffed in their pockets like snippets of old yarn.

That outward concern is also, of course, a way of saying that I am concerned about the ball of yarn in my own pocket and what I will make of it. This book represents, in my own life, two strands of interest that are woven together. Preaching and psychotherapy are probably two of the most important places where religious imagination is integrated with particular life contexts. One works with images and symbols in both settings. One works with particular individuals and stories in both settings. This book represents one attempt at weaving—not the final attempt, not the last word. I have a lot of strands to weave together.

In the summer of 1985, my particular life context was that I realized that I could not put my finger on what the people of my congregation were bringing to worship, much less what they were receiving in worship—a strange question, perhaps. How are people fed? What is nourishing them? I am sure I was also wrestling with my own feeding and nourishment. At the General Assembly of the Christian Church (Disciples of Christ) that summer, I spent a lot of time with my friends Gary and Laura Smith, who had been regaling me with their marvelous stories about the kinds of things that happened in worship when they came down out of the pulpit and talked with people. I had heard of that before but never knew anyone who had actually done it. For whatever reason, I came away ready to try it myself.

And then it happened. Out of the pulpit, I discovered that in preaching, as well as in therapy, people are fed by the value given to their own experience. I have been preaching interactively in the years since, and I continue to find myself nourished as well by the vitality of lived human experience.

Interactive Preaching is the name I have coined for this style of sermon. This book is my attempt to think systematically about both the purpose and the method of preaching outside of the pulpit. It is my attempt to offer some of the possibilities and to warn of some of the pitfalls. It is my challenge for you to reflect on the purpose of preaching. It is my invitation for you to consider new alternatives.

I might just as well have titled this book, "The Psychology of the Sermon." A sermon, as any other pattern of human interaction, is a psychological event. That is to say, the time has come for us to acknowledge that beyond the ritual of proclamation lies the humanity of both the proclaimer and the listener. Beyond the theology of the sermon lies the psychology of the sermonizer, which influences the theology of the sermon in concrete and predictable ways. Beyond the content of what is spoken lie the lives of who is speaking and who is listening. Implicit in interactive preaching is a critique of basic homiletical presuppositions. Implicit are questions about the nature and purpose of ministry. Implicit are concerns for the church in modern life.

Those implications are left as questions. This book is simply the beginning of a conversation about religious dialogue, about the forms that religious language may take in the reality of living on the edge of the twenty-first century. Where that conversation may lead I am not sure. However, I am convinced that the tapestry that each of us weaves from the different strands of images tangled in our faith and in our culture will come from the unique and particular stories of our own experiences.

THE MINSTREL
AND THE HOLY MAN

Preaching from Above or Below

Once upon a time, there was a man who strayed from his own country into the Land of Fools. He saw a number of people flying in terror from a field where they had been trying to reap wheat. "There is a monster in that field," they told him. He looked and saw that it was a watermelon.

He offered to kill the "monster" for them. When he had cut the melon from its stalk, he took a slice and began to eat it. The people became even more terrified of him than they had been of the melon. They drove him away with pitchforks, crying, "He will kill us next, unless we get rid of him."

It so happened that at another time another man also strayed into the Land of Fools, and the same thing started to happen to him. But, instead of offering to help with the "monster," he agreed with them that it must be dangerous and by tiptoeing away from it with them he gained their confidence. He spent a long time with them in their houses until he could teach them, little by little, the basic

1

facts which would enable them not only to lose their fear of melons, but even to cultivate them themselves.[1]

I want to suggest that preaching is not unlike straying into the Land of Fools. It is a land of deep darkness, rich with myth, fear, and terrible monsters. From the point of view of the pulpit, looking down on the Land of Fools, there is a persistent temptation to cut the myth off at its roots. We are trained to demythologize. I remember literally ripping the pages out of a Bible during a sermon in some vague attempt to protest what our love of favorite scriptures and *Reader's Digest* has done to the canon. Like the first stranger into the Land of Fools, I soon found out that symbol is stronger than science. The higher the pulpit, the lower one's vulnerability to watermelon monsters. However, the higher the pulpit, the higher one's vulnerability to pitchforks.

But there is another point of view: a view from below. The second stranger was able to see the watermelon monster from below. From that vantage point, the roots of myth are a beautiful living thing. Sermons in the Land of Fools would be more helpful as spades than as swords.

The height of our pulpits also affects our hearing as much as it affects our vision. As Henri Nouwen reminds us:

> The spiritual leader must first of all be obedient to his [or her] people. The word obedience finds its root in the word *audire*, which means "to hear." Obedient leaders, therefore, must be listeners who are constantly lending an open ear to their people. When they do not they become absurd, which means deaf (*surdus*, deaf). This listening can never happen from a distance but only from within, from a center where the real voices can be heard and discerned. Great spiritual leaders have discovered

[1]Idries Shah, *The Way of the Sufi*. E.P. Dutton & Co., Inc., 1978, p. 207ff.

that by fully entering into the joys and fears of their people, by divesting themselves of all artificial safeguards...they were able to offer a kind of help they could never have imagined from afar. I am not speaking here about a tactic or strategy, but about a spirituality.

...Not critical observation, but compassionate participation: that is the vital source of all authority. This is hard to learn since our defenses against this type of leadership are great.[2]

I suggest that when the pulpit is valued as an elevation from which we talk all the time, we have become absurd—deaf. In the Land of Fools we must learn to preach without talking, because only by bending low enough to truly hear (*audire*) do we become compassionately obedient.

Sadder still, not only does the height of our pulpits affect our vision and hearing but it also profoundly alters our capacity for feeling. When we can no longer see the watermelon monsters our people see, and no longer hear the language our own people speak, we lose our essential feeling connection. We become, in a word, apathetic. Without *pathos*, which in the wisdom of the Greek language means "suffering," we cannot be *co*(m)-*passionate*, meaning "to suffer with." Preaching without passion is literally apathetic. The German language has yet another word play. As Jürgen Moltmann points out, "that is the modern death, called apathy: life without suffering (*das Leiden*) is life without passionate feeling (*das Leidenschaft*)."

What causes us to be so apathetic? What reduces a life so much that one can hardly call it life anymore?

Apathy originally meant freedom from suffering, and in antiquity it was regarded as the highest virtue....Therefore a person had to be free of passionate

[2]Henri Nouwen, "Compassion, the Core of Spiritual Leadership," in *Occasional Papers*, No. 2, March 1977, The Institute for Ecumenical and Cultural Research, p. 1f.

feeling. One had to live without anger, but also without love. Pain and joy could no longer touch one.

...When the passionate devotion to life is missing, the powers to resist (death) are paralyzed. Therefore if we want to live today, we must consciously *will* life. We must learn to love life with such a passion that we no longer become accustomed to the powers of destruction. We must overcome our own apathy and be seized by the passion for life.[3]

If the height of our pulpit leaves us blind, deaf, and apathetic, it will also soon leave us mute. Burnout is an apt metaphor. The fuel is spent, the fire grows cold. Alone in our preaching, there is no fuel to build a new fire. And when the passion is gone, there is literally nothing left to say— all because the height of our pulpit keeps us strangers in the Land of Fools.

Down the Pulpit Steps: A Definition of Interactive Preaching

If we are to preach with insight, powerful language, and passion, we must learn to come down from the pulpit heights. The purpose of preaching has a new perspective from below rather than from above. Although the distance from the pulpit to the pew is only a matter of a few feet, those steps down from the chancel can be the most difficult journey a seminary-trained minister ever has to undertake. The distance between the pulpit and the pew is the distance between a sermon about experience and a sermon experience; between a sermon about the Kingdom and a Kingdom encounter; between a sermon that describes in

[3]Jürgen Moltmann, *The Passion for Life: A Messianic Lifestyle.* Fortress Press, 1978, pp. 19-22.

scholarly detail the various biblical and theological perspectives on transformation, and a sermon that is transformative. Interactive preaching offers us a way to come down from the pulpit. I define an interactive sermon as *any sermon that draws its text, its interpretation of scripture, from the relational experience between the story of scripture and the life context of the listener.* In every interactive sermon there is an openness that invites and elicits response from the congregation during the sermon, as an essential feature of the process of sermonizing. The minister opens the story of the text and invites the listener to proclaim, "This is *my* experience, this is *my* story." The sermon opens itself to that relational moment when the sacred story and the subjective experience confront each other eye to eye.

I remember rushing through one Holy Week only to find myself on Maundy Thursday eye to eye with the congregation at the Last Supper. I stood level with them beside the pews. In this sermon I had laid out the events leading Jesus and the disciples to that upper room, the history and text of the Passover *haggadah*, but instead of outlining my own fantasy of that first eucharist, I asked them what they wanted to say to Jesus in that moment. It felt risky, for I usually want Jesus to remain a theological abstraction, a correct and responsible historical re-construction, a moral and uplifting example. But that night the people there seemed to want just to touch him, just wanted a symbolic presence, not my abstractions.

"What do you want to say to him in this moment?" A woman says: "I want you not to suffer. I want you not to hurt." I think of the theology of redemption, how by his sacrifice humanity is redeemed, so that she can't say that. She can't mean it. And I know it's herself that she projects on Jesus—her suffering, her pain, that she wants to end. But when I ask the second question, "How do you think Jesus would respond to you? What would he say?" she surprises me. "He would say, 'You must not fear to suffer. You must accept your pain, as I bear mine.'" Suddenly this woman speaks the truth to herself and she finds it within herself. And as she speaks it the answer hits home. She has asked, and she has been answered. Deep inside, her symbolic Jesus has spoken to her and said what I would never have been able to say to her eye to eye.

And that night this symbolic Jesus spoke to each and every one present. Their words to him were subjective and far removed from any theology that speaks to humanity "in general." But what he "spoke" to them was subjective as well, bringing a word most intimate and personal and aimed at the heart that spoke from their own experience, their own context. He spoke not as a theological abstraction but as a symbolic reality. A man wanted to say to him, "Have courage, have hope, we are with you," but he answered, "I must walk my road alone, as you must walk yours." Another woman said, "I thank you, I love you, I rejoice in what you are doing for me," and he answered her, "You do not know what I am doing. You do not know the cost." And so it went. I did not catch the psychological complexity of the many dynamics in the sanctuary that night, but I know I witnessed that a word was spoken. I know that a word hit home.

"Relational experience" expresses a complicated cluster of ideas. First, I want to stress the term *relational* because it underlines my conviction that an interactive sermon creates an "I-Thou" relationship. We do not relate to an "it" because the "it" remains essentially a screen for our own psychological projections. We see only the dark shadow hidden from our awareness, conveniently cast on an outer object. If the object cannot carry a projection, we see nothing at all, a dehumanized "it." In any case, we are blinded. And also deaf, for an "it" cannot speak. We hear only the echoes of our inner voices. Because we cannot see or hear it, "it" has no true identity and thus we can have no feeling toward it.

How often do we stand in the pulpit and deliver a sermon to "the congregation"—preach to "it," about "it," for "it"? We imagine that we see, hear, and feel it, when most often our talk about "the congregation" is simply a projection of ourselves. On the other hand, when "it" becomes a beloved "Thou" in the form of a flesh-and-blood individual, our preaching becomes relational. When a unique and particular person stands and responds, we are forced to see an essential "otherness" from ourselves, forced to hear what they say that we would never say. Slowly a distinct identity forms a "Thou" in relationship to "I." As individuals take shape as "Thous," the congregational "it" passes away so that we are able to be in relationship with a community of beloved "Thous," *koinonia* in the best New Testament sense of the word.

The miracle is that in relationship with a "Thou," "I" begin to be truly known. In seeing the otherness of a "Thou," the distinctiveness that makes us each an "I" is also known. In hearing another voice, I know my own voice more fully. "I" am known only in relationship to "Thou." As "Thou" gives "I" an identity, a feeling connection is made. Thus, where once we were known to the congregation as "its" minister, "its" preacher, now a unique and particular human "Thou" emerges from underneath the mantle of the robe. *Interactive preaching creates an "I-Thou" relationship that is transforming both for the congregation and the minister.*

This transformation of relationship necessarily implies a transformation of the language of preaching. Relational experience requires a different way of talking. Here I want to stress the term *experience*. Interactive preaching aims at bringing an experiential "event" quality to the sermon. The interactive sermon generates experience and uses that event as its subject matter. The topic of the sermon is the event of the sermon itself as it is being experienced in the here and now. For the sermon to be that kind of *sprach-erreignis*, a "language-event," language must be transformed to a primary level. Whereas a traditional sermon is secondary language *about* experience, the interactive sermon generates the primary language *of* experience.

Although the distinction between primary language and secondary language is dealt with in the next chapter, let me emphasize now that primary language is the language of story, symbol, metaphor, parable, dreams, myth, and the gospels. It is the language of images arising in the unconscious. It is the undigested language of unique life histories. In an interactive sermon, the biblical story shared by the preacher and the responsive stories shared by the congregation "coalesce." That participatory experience of correspondence between the scriptural story and the life context of the listeners clears the space for an appropriation of the text. In effect, the text becomes a "Thou" and the relational experience is the "coalescence" of the scriptural story and the life context of the listener.

The need for an experiential reality of faith cuts fairly deep. All too often we assume that our preaching speaks out of a shared basis of religious experience, that the traditional references of our faith language touch a common core of experience. We assume that words like "sacrifice," "grace," even "God," are grounded in the living context of people's lives as a vibrant experiential reality. I want to challenge that assumption in two ways. First, we do not really know another person's experience until that person tells it. Oddly enough, we do not particularly "know" our own experience until we tell it, until we bring it to language, until we give it voice. Time and time again in therapy, in the secret conversations between friends, or in the lonely hours writing in a journal, we are surprised at what we say. Unspoken experience—unworked experience, unstoried experience—is unconscious experience. Language is one way in which we integrate the unconscious contents into consciousness where meaning can be born. That is gospel, the "good story." Interactive preaching aims at opening the space for people to interpret, to speak the good story, from their own lives. They speak the common ground between their own stories and the gospel story, and suddenly they know and we know and in the shared life of the congregation we all touch the experience together.

Furthermore, it is not simply that we do not know the experiential reference of faith language until it is told. We cannot even assume the experience. Sermons can be words, important words, with no experiential reference at all. We live in an extraverted age. When life is lived so much on the outside, the essential interiority that makes us open to experience is often lost—the loss of soul. Religious experience requires interiority—requires an interior vessel that, like the holy grail, holds experience up for reflection. Without the grail, the water of life is never tasted. Without our interiority, the word of God, the whisper of God, is drowned in the god of words. We cannot assume people have an opening to religious experience in the way they live their lives. I am suggesting that insofar as we lose the opening to religious experience, we lose the reference of primary religious language. Interactive preaching, then, is an invitation to initiate, encourage, reclaim, and rekindle the value of subjective, interior experience.

Thus, the definition of interactive preaching as a sermon that draws its text, its interpretation of scripture, from the *relational experience* between the story of scripture and the life context of the listener, comes out of my concern for the power of religious language, for the potential inherent in reconnecting words and experience, stories and subjective associations, meaning and living contexts.

On Becoming a Minstrel: Openness to the Relational Experience

Interactive sermons are relational experiences. I certainly experience the birth narratives differently now after inviting several women to share their inner experiences of pregnancy with the congregation in that context. No one had ever asked them to share the things they "pondered in their hearts" as Mary did. And a man told a story about sharing Christmas with an "enemy" family in occupied territory during a war, because there was literally no room for him in the inn. During an All Saints celebration, in response to a question about unusual experiences connected with death, a woman told a story about a flower that blossomed impossibly on the day of her husband's death. A man shared his frustration over a doctor's treatment of his dying mother. Another man shared a funny incident about pallbearers falling into an open baptistry with the casket. We laughed and cried and experienced the mystery of death. One of my favorite memories comes from a sermon on waiting in Gethsemane in which I put the question, "What is the hardest thing you've ever had to do in your life?"—as Jesus might have faced there his most difficult challenge. The variety of responses was inspiring. For one woman there was the memory of the first day of first grade. Several persons mentioned the death of a spouse. One woman told of a day when she and her sister had to confront their father in later life about his relationship with their mother.

We were all, the congregation and I, richer for the stories. They amplified and illumined the text in ways I never could have done. They brought us closer together as the family of God. We knew one another better and had a feel for just how much our stories had in common with one another. They were better "illustrations" than I could consistently think up week after week, because they did not simply "illustrate"—they "participated in" the biblical text.

What usually happens in an interactive sermon is that the proclaimer walks down from the pulpit and chancel to the nave. The sermon might begin with a guided meditation on the scriptural text, with some introductory remarks explaining the interactive sermon process, or with the kind of stories often used as a sermon introduction. Outlines or a prepared text (on small cards) may be used. An interactive sermon may actually be as expository as any other sermon, with one significant difference: In the context of being on the same level as the congregation, eye to eye, the proclaimer asks questions that clearly invite the congregation to respond.

These questions may take the form of asking for a story in which such and such was the situation, and the proclaimer begins with a story of his or her own. Or the questions may go to a set of feelings related to a particular kind of experience. Or the question might invite a dialogue with a scriptural character. As long as the question invites an image or feeling or thought that guides the listener to respond out of his or her own life context, the interactive moment is opened. As the congregation responds, the proclaimer hears and ponders each story, sharing a few comments and weaving the story into the biblical text. Every comment, every story, is valued and given a positive connotation.

There are many variations. An interactive sermon might be as straightforward as a sermon that might otherwise be preached from the pulpit, with the addition of two directed questions (sharply focused). It might be as different as a sermon of shared storytelling around a particular scripture, or a joint musing and discussion of an exegetical point. Whatever the extent of the interaction, an interactive sermon assumes a pattern of *call and response*. This response need not necessarily be verbal, in the first instance, although it seems to me that a sermon cannot be distinctly interactive until there is true dialogue. An interactive sermon need not necessarily be preached from somewhere other than the pulpit, although it seems to me a sermon cannot be truly interactive until it becomes relational. In the long run, an interactive sermon is a relational experience between people who encounter one another on the same level—emotionally, cognitively, socially, and physically in the worship space. The purpose, value, and power of an interactive sermon is a relational experience that opens up space for meaning, *koinonia*, and transformative experience.

Perhaps it would be helpful to describe what the kind of interactive sermon I am talking about is *not*. For instance, an interactive sermon is not a debate between the pastor and the people. Probably we've all had dreams of someone standing up and challenging a sermon. Dreams like that should be an invitation for us to examine what our inner voice is saying about the attitude of our preaching. If in our sermonizing we have essentially closed our interpretation, it probably needs to be challenged. An interactive sermon is not a "set-up," not an opportunity for the divine

word of the preacher to be greeted with a rousing "Amen."
The "relational" quality is lost in the *participation mystique* of the audience with the omnipotent preacher.

Neither is the interactive sermon a talk show interview. Although it may actually resemble a talk show
format, with the proclaimer in the congregation asking
questions and following up, and may quite naturally be
referenced to television by the congregation, there is an
essential difference: My sense of talk shows is that the
stories told by the audience are not inherently valued.

Interactive sermons do not have people talk about
"What does this scripture mean to you?" Although that
question and style might be appropriate in some settings.
It asks people to talk in discursive, secondary language
"about" experience. What an experience means is known
only in the story that gives it a context. Truly interactive
preaching invites people to share experience out of their
own life context, rather than their opinions.

Interactive preaching is not public psychotherapy. I'm
sure that my sense of a relational experience is drawn from
the therapeutic alliance of a psychotherapy relationship.
In the therapeutic alliance, both parties have agreed and
actually act upon a set of boundaries and a focus that are
clearly for the client's benefit. Both the therapist and the
client work hard in the alliance for a common goal. At a
deeper level, the therapeutic alliance serves to restructure
the relational "attitude" of the client because most people in
therapy have not previously experienced relational alliances
that were healing. While those sentences in no way give an
adequate definition of the therapeutic alliance, the same
things could be said of an interactive sermon. Interactive
preaching is like therapy insofar as it creates a therapeutic
alliance between the preacher and the congregation.

Another similarity to psychotherapy has to do with the
"vessel" of therapy. In an adequate alliance—special time,
special place, no contact outside of the context of therapy—
therapy becomes a sealed vessel, a sacred ground, strong
enough to contain the wide range of affects and fantasies
found in therapy. The vessel is the healing atmosphere of

therapy. In the same way, worship provides the vessel that contains and limits the affect-laden stories that the interactive sermon invites. The limiting vessel of worship keeps the atmosphere "therapeutic."

The difference between public psychotherapy and an interactive sermon is the use that is made of the stories. People tell stories in both settings, and I have confidence—from my experience with both—that the depth of the stories heard in an interactive sermon is no less profound than the depth of those told in therapy. But the crucial difference is that in therapy a client must work toward a conscious integration of the meaning of the story (the real work of therapy). An interactive sermon *must* leave that exploration for the psychotherapist (however inviting the clues may be). The stories told in a sermon are essentially amplifications of the biblical story with images, symbols, and experiences of the congregation. The deeper connections remain unconscious or at least a matter for private reflection. Phrased differently, public psychotherapy would move into the realm of secondary, evaluative language. Interactive sermons keep stories in primary language and do not probe beyond that.

The responses I have received to interactive preaching have been varied. The general pattern has been that somewhere between 10 and 20 percent of the congregation will speak up in response to an interactive question—fewer in the beginning, more after a while. But a surprising number of people who do not respond in the sermon often greet me after the worship saying, "You know that question you asked? I would have said...." I feel confident most people ponder an answer to an interactive question or have a story come to mind, whether or not they ever speak.

All in all, I have found that interactive sermons change the scent of worship. The air is different. People experience themselves less as an audience to worship and more as participants. It is a living expression of *liturgy*, "the work of the people." It is a concrete embodiment of the priesthood of all believers. As they hear one important life story after another, there is a growing sense that their own stories are important and valued by the community. One woman put it succinctly: "I used to think that only preachers could preach!" Now she feels she has the good story to tell. Where once the sermon experience was without vision, absurd, and apathetic, as a relational experience it can become insightful, obedient, and truly compassionate. In short, where once there was a stranger in the Land of Fools, there can be joint citizenship in the household of God.

It may very well be that interactive preaching challenges age-old notions of the form and value of sermons, the thrust and goal of sermonic interpretation. In preaching interactively, we confront our homiletic values head on. We give up control over the content of the sermon, because what will be said in the sermon is now out of our hands and we cannot predict how people will respond. We lose our "expert" status as sole authority in scriptural interpretation, expounders of truth, and proclaimers of the gospel, and instead we open ourselves to interpretations that may be quite different from our own. We lose the platform from which to exclaim our vision of the world to a captive audience, and instead we become learners of others' visions of the world. In short, by preaching interactively we lose much of what many preachers fight so hard to maintain. Interactive preaching calls for us voluntarily to displace ourselves not only from the physical space of the pulpit but from the symbolic space that guides our images of preaching.

> The discipline of compassion is displacement, voluntary displacement. Displacement, according to the dictionary, means "to move or shift from the ordinary or proper place...." Voluntary displacement is the discipline necessary to prevent us from being caught in the net of the ordinary and proper....In order for displacement to be a real discipline however, it must be a voluntary displacement, a displacement which we can affirm from within even when we have little or no control over the external circumstances.[4]

[4]Nouwen, "Compassion, the Cord of Spiritual Leadership," p. 3.

Interactive preaching is voluntary displacement. In stepping down from the pulpit, although that simple act in itself has a profound effect on our identity as a preacher, we displace ourselves from many other supports of the role that hold us up. Out of the pulpit, we are displaced from our "expert" stance in which we know something that others need to learn, and are instead confronted with people who know something we do not know but need to learn—their life context. We are also suddenly equals, confronted with preaching out of the same material that others also share—our own life experience. Thus, interactive preaching is a voluntary displacement that challenges us as a creative crisis to revision our image of the proclaimer.

The implication of this method is that the proclamation, the good news, the communication of a sermon, is grounded more in the life context in which the sermon is preached than in the content that is spoken. That is to say, *what is spoken and what is heard cannot be fully realized without also knowing who is speaking and who is listening, without becoming part of a relational experience.* Interactive preaching challenges the notion that meaning is an impersonal value that can be applied regardless of the subjective context: emphasis given to what is said. It implies that meaning is a subjective value that informs and colors the impersonal context: emphasis given to who is speaking. The challenge of interactive preaching lies in its method of interpretation: subjective, life context, relational, experiential.

A story a friend once gave me about the minstrel and the holy man comes to mind.

The Minstrel and the Holy Man:
A Fable by Laura Maynard Smith[5]

Once there was a happy minstrel who traveled through all the kingdom. He carried only his lute,

[5]An unpublished story. Used by permission of the author.

his songs, and his love of laughing people. It may
have been that he was the best minstrel in the
kingdom. People often agreed on that. But he didn't
care for fame. Rather he always traveled on to the
next town, never staying in one place long enough
to become well known.

From village to village and castle to castle his
songs could be heard. He didn't distinguish prince
or pauper. Mirth and meaning were his gifts to all.
It was said that he once clowned his way between
two fighting kings and sang them to peace. It was
said he danced on tavern tables and brought rain to
save the harvest. And his tunes echoed after him on
the lips of the townspeople as he slipped quietly away.

One night there was a terrible rain in the forest.
The minstrel hurried on his path to the next tavern,
shaking the rain from his boots at the door.

But the tavern people were subdued. Above
their cowered heads the minstrel could make out
the voice of a Holy Man. Driven into the society of
tavern people by the rain, the Holy Man preached
to them, demanding that they repent and follow the
high and holy way. The minstrel had heard tell of
this hermit and remembered that he came out of
seclusion from time to time, not to dance or sing, but
to preach. Then he returned to his cave in the woods
to eat his wild berries and herbs. Shaking his head,
the minstrel slipped quietly into the shadows of the
tavern. Appreciating the gifts of human speech, he
found merit in the Holy Man's sermon. The high
rhetoric was moving, but sometimes went beyond
the minstrel. He was stirred only at those places
where the Holy Man's words touched on his own
experience in the wood, castle, and taverns.

The Holy Man's pleas for repentance and threats
of damnation were not well met. The ale had soured
the tavern people's ears and they began to laugh.
When their laughter gave way to rowdiness, the
minstrel stepped in with a song. Everyone, includ-

ing the Holy Man, was anxious for relief and joined in his song. But the Holy Man did not sing. With curious amazement he listened to the first two songs, then quickly left the room.

When the song finished and the tavern people cheered for more ale, the minstrel hurried after the Holy Man. With his black robe pulled close around his head, the Holy Man stood in the doorway, facing the rain. He was grim as he spoke.

"You have set things out of kilter, minstrel," he said. "I am called to set people on the high and holy way and so bring them peace, you to entertain and amuse. Yet they laugh at me, and you bring them peace. Whence comes your wisdom?"

"Wisdom?" The minstrel smiled. "I am a poor minstrel. I have no home. I have no books. You are schooled and a holy man before God. You know the secrets of life. I come to you for wisdom."

"I have only bitterness. You are chosen, minstrel. And blessed. God has set love upon you and in you. I am met only with derision." He turned away.

"Wait, good father. Hear my confession."

"What have you to confess? I see no sin in you. Go your way in peace."

"No, wait." The minstrel caught him in the rain. "I have sinned, father. I was chosen, yes, but I did not choose. Had I given myself to the task I might have been a holy man, like you."

"My life has followed an ancient and honored way. I have spent many years learning the writing of holy things. It is a serious task. Have you any seriousness?"

"Have you any joy, good father?"

"I have the comfort of many years labor."

"Have a game with me," said the minstrel. "Trade your life for mine for one day, you to learn joy, I to learn seriousness."

The Holy Man stopped in the rain. Turning to the minstrel, he frowned.

"My God does not game, minstrel."

"Then let us play in all seriousness."

Reluctantly, the Holy Man agreed. They met the next morning, exchanging the minstrel gown for the holy robe. The minstrel was instructed by the Holy Man in the way of seriousness—to be silent and contemplative, to plea with anyone he met to repent of their evil. The Holy Man was instructed to mingle among the tavern people, singing songs and making them merry even if he had to fool himself at his own expense. They agreed to meet at the tavern after sunset to compare experiences.

The minstrel wandered through the woods, contemplating holy, serious thoughts, trying to look priestly whenever people passed nearby. Finally he spoke to some hunters, telling them of their evil nature and urging them to make absolution in the parish church. In all of this he was highly dissatisfied, but he wanted to play the game fairly.

At sunset the minstrel returned to the tavern, anxious to tell the Holy Man of his learning. The lesson had been simple enough—compared with the life of the Holy Man, the minstrel would choose his own calling. He felt his sin absolved.

But evening darkened into night. The minstrel paced the floor, fearful that some danger had befallen the Holy Man. Then he had a strange, peaceful thought. Through the rest of the night he waited and slept, waking to find the bench beside him empty and the sun rising gold and glorious. Smiling, he discarded the Holy Man's robes and went on his way singing.

The people of the kingdom were delighted whenever either of the two wandering minstrels came to their village with joy and music.

GROUNDING
INTERACTIVE PREACHING

Theological Grounding

I approach a sermon with one overarching assumption: *Experience transforms, description informs.* People need both transformation and information at various milestones in life. People need both the sheer power of life as it is experienced, and a reflective description of that experience so that they can organize and understand its meaning. Sermons can perform both functions, but probably not at the same time. Descriptions of experience (reports, analyses, lectures, theologies, sermons) are not on the whole transformative. Sheer, raw, undigested experience (birth, death, love, abandonment) in the moment of its epiphany is not on the whole informative. Instead, in the moment of experience we know only a state of being (confusion, awe, renewal, despair). Description puts back together what experience has pried open.

Experience transforms, description informs. Underlying my basic assumption is a set of convictions about the structure of language.

I remember one of my parishioners telling me in hushed tones about an experience she had in the recovery room after a surgery. She said that coming up out of the anesthesia, out of the unconscious, she had seen something in her

19

body. "It was like a living red line." She was trembling as she said it. "And I have an idea I was seeing my soul." She had no idea, I think, of the symbolic history of the soul image. In fact, in the Middle Ages the soul was sometimes described as a thin red line stretched between our life and eternity. I told her, yes, there she had seen her soul.

Very often when people are trying to describe an intense or unique experience, they grope for metaphors and analogies. Sheer, raw experience often goes beyond the boundaries of everyday language, and metaphor is the only way to commmunicate it. Heidegger called that the "language of Being," primordial or primary language. Primary language is characterized by a close connection between the linguistic description of the event and the event itself. This connection is so close we might call this form of language *event-language*: The experience described by the language happens again in the hearing. It briefly opens a window into the house of being. "The user of language is alive," says Phillip Wheelwright, "and accordingly as he lives with intensity his thoughts and utterances require language that can express their living form."[1]

When life is lived with intensity, language necessarily takes on that form. Primary language is a language of presence, language connected to reality at such a deep level that the experience is present in the language. This happens through a *memesis*, i.e., it mimics reality at such a profound level that the relationships and connections in the language itself parallel the relationships and connections between things in reality. Such a correspondence between language and experience is possible because the symbolic nature of primary language links raw experience with a history of the way parallel experiences have been imaged in the past. Consciously or unconsciously, our metaphors have a symbolic history. For example, a description of the soul in primary language "constellates" (to use a psychological term) the experience of soul within each of us.

[1]Phillip Wheelwright, *Metaphor and Reality*. Indiana University Press, 1962, p. 17.

There is another way of speaking about soul. We could talk about the soul by reviewing the doctrine of the soul from the early church to the present. In precise language one could talk about the various theological issues associated with soul, or do a word study contrasting the various uses of the term in the period of the Enlightenment and nineteenth-century Romanticism. We call that kind of language "secondary language." It is language *about* experience. If primary language is characterized by its connection to experience, then secondary language is characterized by its connection with the human passion for order— a connection with some universal ordering principle. Secondary language is rational and logical. Connections and similarities metaphorically shown in primary language are ordered and described in secondary language. Thus it is the language of concepts and systems. It lacks the presence of primary language, but attempts to describe experience in great detail. It makes experience understandable and intelligible.

If primary language is the language of seeing, then secondary language is the language of reflection, re-viewing what primary language has already seen. If primary language can be said to invite us into new experience, secondary language can be said to order what we already know. The one is full of metaphor, symbol, story, and myth. The other finds expression in concept, ideas, theses, and systems.

There is no "absolute qualitative distinction" between primary language and secondary language. They exist on a continuum from incomprehensible schizophrenic delusions to bicycle-assembly instructions in three languages. Both become grids through which we sift our experience of the world. Both are alike, yet unlike.

Primary language is the language of poets, founders of religions, and schizophrenics. Secondary language is the language of scientists, advertisers, and neurotics, as well as most theologians and preachers.

There's the rub. Most of us have grown up with and have been taught in seminary to write sermons in secondary language. In the range of most of our experience, secondary language is the only expression a sermon could (and should) take. We assume that our listeners share a faith that is rooted in key traditions that all American Christians share, and thus our preaching becomes the task of organizing and making sense of our common experience. In truth, I believe there is actually no such common base of religious *tradition*. What we share is a very human stock of *experience*. If that is the case, then our sermons about tradition are simply serving up the dressing, but there is no turkey on the table. Everybody finds the meal unsatisfying after a while. It's the meat of raw experience that feeds us. We also assume our listeners make the connection between the experiences in the story of scripture and the experiences in their own life stories. In truth, I believe we often mistake a rational connection made in the head for a feeling (experiential) connection made with our whole being. Therein lies all the difference in the world: the difference between faith as a way of *thinking about* life, and faith *as a way of life*.

Experience transforms, description informs. Interactive preaching is a conscious, intentional method of revitalizing the experiential basis of faith. Rather than assuming a common basis of religious experience, interactive preaching sets out to create it. Rather than assuming people make the connection from scripture to life in their heads, interactive preaching invites them to make the connection with each other. Interactive preaching aims at creating a sermon from the primary language of experience, rather than from secondary descriptions and interpretations of experience.

Primary language, of course, is the language of the gospel: story, metaphor, parable. The sayings of Jesus do not read like a theology book. The language of the earliest Christians is extravagant, paradoxical, shocking, and full of a tension between opposites, precisely because what they experienced contained just those qualities. The form of the gospel language is intrinsically related to the nature of the gospel experience.

And what was the nature of that experience? Something obviously happened to those people. Shepherds were the first to hear the angels' announcement. Fishermen became religious authorities. Housekeepers and prostitutes were the first to discover an empty tomb. The son of a carpenter became present in the breaking of bread.

Religious experience is as old as the strange paintings in the hidden caves of Lascaux and as contemporary as Christian television. It has always been controversial in the Christian church, the controversy beginning probably before the founding of the church in Corinth. It has alternately been valued and repressed. Rudolph Otto gave us the classical description of religious experience:

Let us consider the deepest and most fundamental element in all strong and sincerely felt religious emotion...*mysterium tremendum*. The feeling of it may at times come like a sweeping gentle tide, pervading the mind with a tranquil mood of deepest worship. It may pass over into a more set and lasting attitude of the soul, continuing as it were, thrillingly vibrant and resonant, until at last it dies away and the soul resumes its "profane," non-religious mood of everyday experience. It may burst in sudden eruptions from the depth of the soul with spasms and convulsions, or lead to the strangest excitements, to intoxicated frenzy, to transport, and to ecstasy. It has wild and demonic forms and can sink to an almost grisly horror and shuddering. It has its crude, barbaric antecedents and early manifestations, and again it may be developed into something beautiful and pure and glorious. It may become hushed, trembling, and speechless humility of the creature in the face of—whom or what? In the presence of that which is a *Mystery* inexpressible and above all creatures.[2]

For all of Otto's nineteenth-century language and world view, that description is still very accurate. We

[2]Rudolph Otto, *The Idea of the Holy*, translated by John W. Harvey. Oxford University Press, 1923, p. 12f.

encounter the Holy on an emotional level with feelings of awe, terror, and fascination. Most importantly, Otto recognized the religious experience as a relational encounter with *Otherness*, the great mystery. Giles Gunn gives a more modern definition of religious experience that makes this relational encounter explicit:

A solitary self...falls, so to speak, into experience and encountering there that ideal "Other" in response to which he must, at the minimum, redefine himself and, at the maximum, virtually recreate himself. Whether the ideal "Other" confronts him in the form of God, the wilderness, Nature, other selves, history, the city, or the machine, man's chief aim in response to this "Other" is neither, at least initially, to try to define it nor, necessarily, to enter into relationship with it. Though both of these things may follow as a consequence, the essential purpose of man's encounter with "Otherness" is to compel him however he responds—whether with love, despair, submission, recoil, outrage, or awe—into some new understanding of and relationship to himself. The desired goal, whether successfully achieved or tragically frustrated, is deliverance and new life, and the method is always some form of *decreation* a sloughing off of the old ways in response to encounter with something astonishingly new.[3]

The relational encounter with Otherness is the nature of religious experience. In that encounter, "I" am redefined in relationship to a "Thou." In my own terms I would point to the intense dislocation the ego encounters when it must acknowledge, in the face of the mysterious Other, that it is not the center of life. That reorientation of the ego as a branch, rather than the vine, so to speak, is the decreation (and recreation) Gunn mentions.

[3]Giles Gunn, *The Interpretation of Otherness*. Oxford University Press, 1979, p. 9.

The gospel as a religious experience is a relational encounter as well, with the same characteristics. The particular nature of Christian experience lies in the distinctive quality of its relational experience: Kingdom encounter. As Otherness, the Kingdom takes on the qualities of the *mysterium tremendum*, yet by the very nature of the Kingdom, the mystery is not on the mountaintop but in everyday life. If we turn to the gospel stories of Jesus' ministry, we see the amazing appearance of the everyday in sacred literature. In classical traditions, sacred themes appear in the realm of the gods, seldom in the profane world. But the gospel is a comedy of simple people—those shepherds, fishermen, housekeepers, prostitutes, and carpenters. In the midst of the most ordinary of the ordinary, there are alarming pictures of the most extraordinary experiences. Jesus' parables are fused with exaggerated circumstances and an extravagance of detail. The parable, while "drawn from nature or common life, [arrests] the hearer by its vividness or strangeness."[4] Exaggeration and extravagance are the marks of the extra-ordinary coming into ordinary life, the marks of the incarnation.

The advent of the kingdom is at once utterly awesome and awesomely normal....Certain actions which all at once seem inevitable and necessary *fill familiar beliefs and former ideas to the bursting point with new and unforeseen meaning.* Life suddenly releases some of its unspent force, and conventional expectations and interpretations are toppled by the flood of new insight and illumination.[5]

That is the nature of the gospel experience: something awesome in the midst of something normal, some mysterious Otherness in the midst of our deepest selves, something divine incarnate in human flesh. Those are the two terms of the relational experience.

[4]C. H. Dodd, *The Parables of the Kingdom*, revised edition. Charles Scribners & Sons, 1961, p. 5.
[5]John Dominic Crossan, *In Parables*. Harper and Row, 1973, p. 53f.

I think now we are able to see the larger issues in defining interactive preaching as a sermon that draws its text, its interpretation of scripture, from the relational experience between the story of scripture and the life story of the listener. Interactive preaching is grounded in the primary language of experience because that is the form of gospel language. Interactive preaching is explicitly relational because that is the nature of the gospel experience. The gospel is the mystery of something awesome speaking in the midst of life's normalcy, and in interactive preaching we strive to let the mystery speak from the gospel stories through the common, everyday life stories of the people in our congregation. Preaching in this way grounds the sermon in the form and nature of the gospel.

I have said that the interactive sermon draws its interpretation of scripture from the relational experience. Most of us, however, were trained to interpret scripture according to the prevailing historical-critical methods of the day. We have probably equated the art of interpretation with the historical-critical method. Thus, interactive preaching requires a new understanding of the methodology of biblical interpretation.

The great service done by the historical-critical method is the way in which it guards us against the danger of reading ourselves into the text. The claim of the method is that it provides us sufficient "distance" to approach the text "objectively." However, in its ever-present fear of what we might do to the text, the historical-critical method of interpretation has also safely insulated us against what the text might do to us.

The crux of the matter is that the historical-critical method *itself* is grounded in the very kind of historical value system from which it promises to liberate us. As Walter Wink reminds us, "detached neutrality in matters of faith is not neutrality at all, but already a decision against responding. At the outset, questions of truth and meaning have been excluded, since they can only be answered participatively, in terms of a lived response."[6] It presupposes that meaning lies in historical clarity and can be objective and neutral. Perhaps this is a holdover from late nineteenth century rational materialism, but in the closing years of the twentieth century we find ourselves in a new paradigm, a psychological paradigm. Our difficulties lie not so much in understanding the *Sitz in Leben* of the text; our difficulty lies in understanding the *Sitz in Leben* of ourselves. Having overvalued the need for objectivity, we have suddenly found ourselves at a loss for ways of finding the meaning of our own subjectivity.

Interactive preaching sets out to stand against a detached, value-neutral, ahistorical interpretive method. From the beginning, the method of interactive preaching is already a commitment to asking people to make subjective judgments and give themselves over to a participative involvement with the text. It asks people to make an interpretation of the text from the life story of their own experience, rather than from the canons of the historical-critical method. It asks them to "wager" an interpretation where the stakes are participation versus isolation, rather than detached objectivity versus subjectivity. Interactive preaching is a commitment to an "appropriation" of the text.

By "appropriation," I am describing the experience by which the text enters into my world: my history, my purpose, my way of seeing myself in the world, and ultimately my way of life. The text becomes the lens through which my life is interpreted. At the beginning of the interpretative process, my world was clearly the subject. But through appropriation, when the text enters my world, suddenly it is my own life that is held up as the object of scrutiny by the text. In the long run, appropriation determines the measure to which we are able to make a commitment to the text, an interpretive "wager" about how we live a life well.

"To appropriate is to make 'one's own' what was 'alien,'" as Riceour says, to bridge "the otherness that

6Walter Wink, *The Bible in Human Transformation: Towards a New Paradigm of Biblical Study.* Fortress Press, 1980, p. 2.

transforms all spacial and temporal distance into cultural estrangement and the ownness by which all understanding aims at the extension of our self-understanding."[7] In fact, appropriation may not lead to the extension of our current self-understanding at all, but to its demise and recreation.

Appropriating, rather than simply understanding, is the goal of interpretation and thus of preaching as well. The gospel aims at completion in the lives of its audience, not at the understanding of it on its own terms in its own world. The gospel falls on our ears, as Jesus parables, with the "necessity of interpretation," as Mary Ann Tolbert calls it.[8] The interpretation of the gospel is not complete until we make a response.

Since the metaphor gives itself existentially to unfinished reality, so that the narrative is not complete until the hearer is drawn into it as participant, the hearer is confronted with a situation in relation to how he must decide how to comport himself: is he willing to allow himself to be victim, to smile at the affront to the priest and the Levite, to be served by an enemy? The parable invites, nay, compels him to make some response....Every hearer has to hear it in *his* own way. The future which the parable discloses is the future of every hearer who grasps and is grasped by his position in the ditch. [9]

Interactive preaching offers us a way to let people speak from their position in the ditch. In a way that a sermon preached only by the proclaimer cannot do, an interactive sermon compels the listeners to complete the interpretation of the gospel by making a response from their life story. It

[7]Paul Riceour, *Interpretation Theory: Discourse and the Surplus of Meaning*. Texas Christian University Press, 1976, p. 43.

[8]Mary Ann Tolbert, *Perspectives on the Parables: An Approach to Multiple Interpretations*. Fortress Press, 1979. (See p. 49.)

[9]Robert Funk, quoted by Norman Perrin in his *Jesus and the Language of the Kingdom*. Fortress Press, 1976, p. 139.

compels them to appropriate the text by getting their life all mixed up with the life of the text. Like Jesus' parables, both the text itself and the life of the hearer are seen in new ways as a result of the "congruence" of the two stories.

Thus, interpretation may be said to be an interactive process, a relational experience in which the correspondence between the story of scripture and the life story of the hearer produces a widening of horizons for both. In interactive preaching we set out to make that process explicit and conscious and communally shared, rather than leaving it unspoken in the mind of the listener.

How do we achieve the interpretive goal of appropriation? Over the past twenty years a good deal of work on such hermeneutical questions has been done that offers a variety of methods. I would suggest a model along the lines of Riceour's theory of aesthetic interpretation.

Aesthetic experience and religious experience have long been twin sisters. I propose that in the same way in which a work of art so arrests our attention through an image of such ingenuity, or beauty, or interest that it leads us "into itself," so a biblical text or sermon might begin the interpretive process by claiming the *rapt attention* of its audience. Serious attention to a work of art or a sermon results in *participation*. Participation means that now the work of art or the sermon takes on an experiential aspect. The work calls to mind, or "accesses," pieces of our own experience. Participation in the work means that a part of myself is now brought into dialogue with the work—a shared story, a recognized image, an underlying correspondence from art to life. That felt *correspondence* is the third step of the interpretive process. As I begin to see my own story side by side with another story, then the similarities and differences between the two create a true dialogue. How might my story be different if it were to follow the form of this story? How might how I see be different were I to see life as this image sees it? Why does this story take one turn when my story takes another turn?

This correspondence, or congruence, or "coalescence" of the art and life is the essential connection that makes *appropriation*, the fourth and final step of this process, possible. As a result of the parallel between my story and the text's story, I have to come to terms with the possibilities that the text suggests are there for me. I have to respond to the text out of my own life situation.

Therefore, I am proposing a four-stage model of interpretation consisting of rapt attention, participation, correspondence, and appropriation. An interactive sermon generates this process in the following way.

The sermon begins with a serious effort to command attention. Sometimes this might be done with a guided meditation on the text, a shared communal reading, or a story told by the preacher. A more traditional introduction and exposition of the text might also command sufficient attention. Next we begin the process of participation with an interactive question that invites people to share something from their own life context. This is the essential feature of participation in the text and in the sermon. If the interactive questions are properly focused and emerge naturally from the text, the correspondence between the responses and the text should be evident. Moving toward the end of the sermon, we then want to ask a question that in one way or another invites people to wrestle with appropriation.

Let us consider an example. In a sermon on the birth narratives, we might ask, "Mothers, can you tell us something about the fears you experienced during pregnancy?" Such a question invites participation, not just on the part of those mothers who respond to the question but also on the part of everyone listening to what the mothers are saying. It also enters imaginatively into the Lukan text (1:26–38) in a way that illumines the motif of fear in chapters one and two. The correspondence is at an experiential level, Mary's and the mothers' fear. But in the end we need to invite an appropriation of the text in a specific way. Thus we might ask, "How are you in a 'pregnant' moment right now?" With that question the angel's announcement of pregnancy comes to the participants in the sermon, as well as to Mary, and the wrestling with the appropriation of being "greatly troubled with the saying" begins. The sermon has moved from discourse on the many historical-critical difficulties with the passage to an experience of annunciation.

Experience transforms, description informs. Sermons need to do both. With that guideline, we begin grounding interactive preaching in biblical theology. Interactive preaching emphasizes the experiential, primary forms of language because such was the form of the language of the gospel. Interactive preaching aims at relational experience because the nature of the religious experience described in the gospel is relational. Finally, the very language and nature of the gospel compels us to interpret the gospel in a way that is appropriate to our life context. Thus, appropriation becomes the goal of interpretation and the heart of the interactive process.

Such a theological understanding of preaching profoundly challenges and alters the paradigms most of us grew up with and learned in seminary. The proclaimer is no longer a junior professor teaching from the pulpit. The proclaimer is no longer in an expert stance, guarding the mysteries of the scripture. The sermon itself is no longer a revelation of knowledge to which only the proclaimer has access, but it becomes an attempt to discover meaning in the life experiences that we all access subjectively. The meaning, when it comes, is subjective. It can never be predicted beforehand, and is not known by either the proclaimer or the listeners except in the moment of its speaking.

I am suggesting that "meaning" as lived, "meaning" as subjectively experienced, is more of an act of imagination than an act of cognition, more a perception of symbolic overtones than a deduction of concrete facts. The art of an interactive interpretation requires the engagement of significant imagination. Faith is our own subjective participation in mythic imagination. As in the parables of Jesus, the interpretation of a text is not complete until the listener makes a lived response, until the listener enters into the images of the text through the door of his or her own imagination. We live the meaning from the inside, and that is the transformation. As long as we stand outside the door, we are stuck with information. That there is a treasure in a field may be informative. But when, through the subjective imagination, there is a treasure in the field *for me*, there can be transformation.

Thus I think that, in the long run, interactive preaching requires not only a new methodology of biblical interpretation, but also a new hermeneutic: the hermeneutic of imagination. From the beginning, the method of interactive preaching is already a commitment to asking people to give themselves over to an imaginative involvement with the text. I say "imagination" because the only way I can enter a story, a biblical story or my own personal story, is through imagination. The only way for the text or my life to open itself to becoming more than it seems to be is through imagination. I maintain that the goal in interpretation is precisely that opening to something more. Meaning is a subjective act of imagination. The meaning of a text, the treasure in the field, is found in the "appropriation" through which we take the text into our own story. Interactive preaching is the invitation for individuals of the congregation living in particular contexts to enter the story, tell the story, share the story. Through that imaginative discourse, they are saying: "My life is more than it seems to be."

I realize that we are not accustomed to thinking of our sermons as invitations to imagination, or of an interpretation as an act of imagination. In fact, we are trained to be suspicious of imagination when it comes to dealing with biblical texts. Insofar as we are trained to demythologize, we are taught to distrust the mythic imagination. However, I cannot think of any way to be religious except through the imagination. I cannot think of any way to participate in a ritual without imagination. I cannot think of any way to be in community without shared imagination. Therefore, I wonder if the time has come to think of the sermon as an attempt to restore the religious imagination of people who are crying out for meaning in a profane world.

Psychological Grounding

As a relational experience, interactive preaching is interpersonal and intrapsychic, so that we move into the psychological. There have been three distinct ways of thinking psychologically that have influenced my understanding of interactive preaching: Jungian (analytic) psychology, neurolinguistic programming, and strategic (or paradoxical) family therapy. In this section, I want to explore some of the psychological ideas that inform interactive preaching.

Carl Gustav Jung (1875-1961) knew a lot about preaching. Not only was his father a practicing parish minister, but no less than eight of his uncles were also parsons. Jung was interested in that connection between experience and language all of his life. Beginning already with his word-association experiment in 1904-5, he noticed that certain words were associated with certain feelings in each individual and that, furthermore, there was a connection between sets of various affective words that he called a feeling-toned complex.

A complex of associations and feelings is an important idea for interactive preaching. A complex is the cluster of feelings, images, symbols, or ideas that are unconsciously related to each other around a central issue. A complex is thus a field, like a magnetic or a gravitational field, that encompasses all the associations connected with it. Once the field is charged, or "constellated," interactions between the various images or elements tend to happen in patterned ways. Jung found this to be true of unique, personal complexes, as well as collective, universally human complexes (which he called "archetypes").

When we approach the psychology of a sermon, the first consideration has to do with the nature of the field or complex that is constellated. I want to offer a vastly simplified model. Think of the intrapsychic field of the listener as laid out in four overlapping levels.

The first and most immediate level could be named the *persona* level, i.e., the mask that each of us presents to the outer world. The persona is the social adaptation all of us have made based upon our personal histories and roles in life—the way we present ourselves to strangers and acquaintances, the way we are *expected* sometimes to present ourselves. Persons in ministry, obviously, are confronted with a variety of expectations about how they present themselves in the role of "the minister." Technically, the persona would be the personal adaptation each of us makes to the role of minister, our own way of wearing the robe.

Just below that level would be a complicated mixture of the subjective factors in a human life, which I will call the *life context* level. This would include on the surface the conscious situations and attitudes that form the context of our life—the stresses and pains of job, family, marriage, aging, etc. These are the kinds of issues we talk about when the pressure is great, or when the trust is at the right level, and the kinds of issues we don't talk about in mixed company. They go against the persona. However, just below these conscious issues lie the kind of complications and "complexes" that unconsciously shape our life and feelings every day, complexes that could be made conscious with some reflection—something like the issues we might become aware of in therapy. Both the conscious and unconscious issues define our life context.

But a human life is patterned in still deeper ways. The third level of the intrapsychic field might be called the *symbolic* level. Our life is patterned not only by subjective psychological factors but also by more impersonal factors. This was Jung's important discovery. He called these archetypal or symbolic patterns. We may, for instance, be living out the instinctual pattern of initiation at a given point in our life (mid-life perhaps), or confronting the shadow (the excluded, disdained elements of our personality), or integrating the anima (the feeling/relational factor of a man) or animus (the ideational/inspirational factor of a woman), or identifying with the wise old man and earth mother. There are many symbolic patterns. At this level we are usually quite unaware of these influences in our life, but the patterns are there nevertheless.

Finally, at the deepest level there is an integrating factor, a grand organization of the personality that Jung called the Self. I want to call this the *core* level of the intrapsychic field. The core of the human personality is a mystery, for we do not know how far and how deep the unconscious extends. We know only that from time to time there is a conscious perception of an unfolding process, which Jung called *individuation*, that goes beyond the ego's will and volition. This perception is experienced sometimes in dreams, perhaps with symbols of the square or the circle (and perhaps not), or sometimes in certain peak experiences.

So we might think of the psychology of the sermon as having to do with the field that is constellated by the interaction between the proclaimer and the listener, something like this diagram:

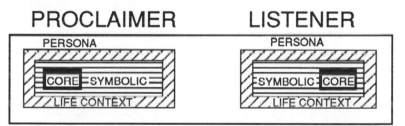

The psychological field or "complex" generated by the sermon is the pattern in which different levels of the proclaimer and the listener are constellated. For instance, a typical constellation might be the proclaimer and the listener engaging each other at the persona level. The field generated by the sermon is at the level of a social interaction, minister and listener engaging in their expected roles. A different kind of field would be constellated, for instance, insofar as the sermon might come more out of the proclaimer's life context level. That is to say, depending on the level of self-disclosure—a personal story or real-life struggle that is shared—the sermon might engage the persona or life context level in the listener in this manner:

PROCLAIMER   LISTENER

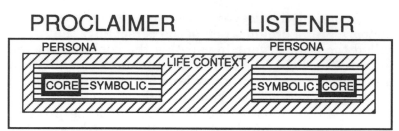

A variety of combinations is possible. Obviously, this is an oversimplification of the psychological field that a sermon generates. These layers are not clear and distinct, but infuse one another in surprising ways. The life context level shapes the persona level in subtle ways. For instance, I remember an Easter sermon in which the proclaimer's focus on the text in John 20:1–18 was verse 10: "Then the disciples returned to their homes." Where we choose to place our emphasis on the texts with which we work often comes out of our own life context. So even though at the persona level the sermon spoke to the traditional Easter message, the life context of this proclaimer, beginning a new pastorate, leaked through: He wanted to go home. In the same way, the symbolic level is always just underneath the stories we tell out of our life context. Insofar as we "story" our experience, we disclose the meaning in underlying symbolic patterns. That's the value of storytelling: It engages the symbolic. And the core level echoes in each and every pattern. It is there all the time.

The model I am offering—persona, life context, symbolic, and core levels—is simply an abstraction. Subjectively experienced, none of these levels is quite so cut and dried. However imperfect, this model offers us at least an image of the various levels a sermon can engage. And we have to beg the question. We assume that the sermon experience, as any experience, generates a psychological field. We might question the particulars of how the field is constituted, but we cannot avoid the insight that patterns of interaction must be present anytime we step into the pulpit.

There is a third factor to add to this dynamic. Not only proclaimers and listeners but even biblical texts have "complexes" as well. A scriptural story such as a parable, while "multivalient" (open to multiple meanings and interpretations), is nevertheless limited to a given set of associations. The story or parable also creates an interpretive field or "complex," which also can be said to have different levels. Medieval scholastic theology talked about four levels of interpreting a text: literal, allegoric, symbolic, and spiritual. We might describe the levels of the text in more modern terms: literal, historical, symbolic, and core. We will illustrate this quartet by reference to the parable of the good Samaritan in Luke 10:30–37.

At the *literal* level, the text speaks with its traditional references. One preaches on the parable by emphasizing the lack of compassion shown by the priests and Levites and the need for us all to be good Samaritans: "Go and do likewise." That's what scripture "says," no "interpretation" necessary. Scripture makes a commandment or gives a mission, and one goes out and does it—the literal level of the text.

The next level might be called the *historical* level of the text. In many ways the historical-critical method is an allegorical interpretation of scripture, understanding the reference of scripture as being the *Sitz in Leben*, or the historical situation of the text, and making the translation, point by point, from the text to the history. That's how allegory works. For instance, we can translate the parable of the good Samaritan point by point into the historical situation of the Lukan community. Form criticism tells us that the story of the question of eternal life (10:25–28) and the parable itself were originally independent units. Why does the writer weave them together? Redaction criticism tells us that insofar as the Lukan community represents the Christian apology to the Greek world after the fall of Jerusalem in A.D. 70, Christians (the "good" Samaritans) are portrayed to cultured Romans as a benevolent, caring, nonviolent people, in contrast to the presentation of Jewish faith (priests and Levites) as insensitive, uncaring, and culturally separate. It is almost as if the gospel writer's use of the story of the fulfillment of the Jewish law in 10:25ff. had to be followed with a statement saying essentially, "Be more than Jewish." Thus the editorializing: "Go and do likewise"—i.e., go and be different. The story and cast of characters have an entirely different slant in a different, pre-gospel historical setting in which the parable represents an intra-faith dialogue in Judaism about the priestly and prophetic fulfillment of the law. The historical level of the text is the parallel to the life context level of the listener/proclaimer, the first speaking out of the particular circumstances of the unique history of the text and the second speaking out of the personal history of the listener/proclaimer.

Yet beyond the demythologized setting of the text, there is a *symbolic* level, a mythological history. The reference of the text is not only to a particular history but to a particular correlation of images, not only to a historical situation but to a universally human pattern: the symbolic level of the text. For instance, in the parable of the good Samaritan the symbolic pattern would include the journey/development motif (individuation issues), the relationship to the shadow aspects of the personality ("enemies" like robbers, Samaritans, etc.), and the relationship to authority (priests, Levites). Century after century, human beings have encountered the road, the enemy, and the priest time and time again, so that the universal human experience that underlies our unique personal experience is also a part of the complex.

At the symbolic level we might consider the parable of the good Samaritan as dream, rather than as biblical text, and interpret the story as that of a man who dreamed he was on the road from Jerusalem to Jericho and fell among robbers. Journeying on a road has the association of movement through the stages of life. Thus we could say that the dreamer is likely to encounter difficulties on the next "passage" on life's road (the robbers). The dreamer turns to different images of traditional religious values (priests and Levites), who are not able to offer any help with his difficulty in completing the journey. It is his enemy, or shadow, who offers help. The shadow can be thought of as the personification of the aspects of ourselves that we have neglected and repressed in the formation of our conscious personalities. Thus, for the dreamer to successfully complete the journey through the next stage of life, the dreamer will have to come to terms with unconscious parts of the personality which up until this stage have been repressed (the Samaritan). From the parable/dream, apparently the shadow is quite willing to provide this help.

Finally, the text also speaks at some *core* level beyond all the others—not in the sense of the historical "kernel" of biblical criticism but rather as an ontological statement, a "status in reality." Here we move into theology. How is the structure of the text at the same time a revelation of the structure of "reality"? For instance, perhaps it can be said that the core of the good Samaritan has to do with the revelation that at some times in our life (on the road), our experience of God comes not from the daylight world (Jerusalem) or from outer religious structures (priests), but from the darker aspects of the personality—the shadow (Samaritan).

Thus, as an initial exploration of the psychology of the sermon, *I propose that we think of the psychological field (the "complex" of the sermon) generated in the experience as the pattern of interaction among the various levels of the proclaimer, the listener, and the text.*

For instance, the following graphic depicts a field generated by the penetration of the symbolic level of the proclaimer into the historical layer of the text and the life context layer of the listener—as, for example a man in mid-life preaching out of his wrestling with the darker aspects of his personality, coming to terms with his shadow. The power of that experience, the fear of that encounter, might be pushing him to steer clear of those personal issues by choosing to deal with the text at an objective, historical level. But the listener sensitive to the body language and emotional tone of the sermon might very well pick up on the apparent intensity of the sermon. Something is going on in this man's life. That intensity in turn constellates those stresses and pressures in the listener's life context.

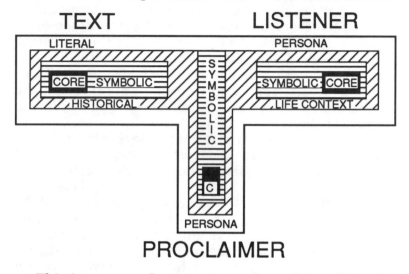

TEXT   LISTENER

PROCLAIMER

This is one way, however imperfect, of describing the pattern of interaction in such a sermon. Another pattern might be something like the minister at her persona level opening the text only as far as its literal level, while the listener, due to a particular personal history perhaps unknown even to him, finds himself strongly moved at the symbolic level.

This is to say, at a minimum, that the psychological experience of a sermon goes far beyond the words actually spoken and includes a complex field of associations and interactions. As people hear the parable, in our example, the field also includes the variety of personal associations and feelings connected to the images and to the parable itself. The personal associations linked together in the complex would include memories and feelings from early years with parents and Bible school and preachers that are connected to hearing that parable, as well as personal experiences of being on the road, robbers, priests, etc. Those complexes are there in every worship service, just

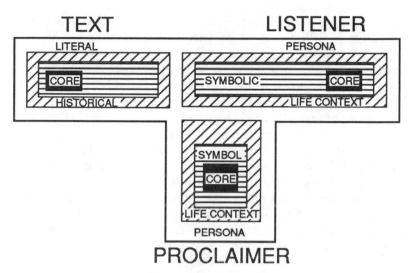

PROCLAIMER

underneath conscious awareness. In fact, those complexes are there in every moment, in every relationship, in every sermon.

Interactive preaching is the attempt to allow more consciously and intentionally for that field to be expressed and explored—to access more fully the different levels in the proclaimer, the listener, and the text. The promise of this method lies in dialogue that more fully opens the life context and symbolic levels. The connection from level to level, from text to proclaimer to listener, is made as a result of the patterns and structure of the images by the field of the complex. We will return to this model later, for further exploration. Suffice it to say here that the questions posed in an interactive sermon invite those connections to be explored consciously.

Jung found that the key to understanding the complexes represented in our dreams was to begin consciously to grasp and experience the connection from one image to another, from the "text" of the dream to the life context of the dreamer. Those connections are called "associations." Associations to dream images are both personal and collective. Remember that as a result of the complex, the field of associations is automatically limited. Each association reveals a fuller aspect of the complex. Slowly, as the associations begin to reveal the broader structure of the complex (in the dream), a meaningful interpretation begins to form. No interpretation is ever really finished, because the field of associations is so large and changes over time.

Jung also found that the process of opening up the field of the dream through association is a helpful interpretive method for opening the field of a story or fairy tale as well. Technically, one associates to a dream; one *amplifies* a story, such as the good Samaritan. The amplification is both personal and collective. We've already mentioned some of the collective elements in the good Samaritan story. I can also amplify the parable personally, remembering just how often the life commandment came to me, "Be a good Samaritan!" When I try to live that out, I find myself uncomfortable with the broken man beside the road. I think of helping those in need as derelicts, although it's not in the parable. Or is it? Clearly in Jesus' parable, the audience identifies with the victim, and the Samaritan enemy is the one they would find uncomfortable. But in our Christian culture, most of us identify with the Samaritan, and not surprisingly our shadow is projected onto the victim. Thus, even when our culture has reversed the characters with whom we usually identify, the shadow element of the complex is still working in our experience of the parable.

There is more than enough material in these amplifications for an interesting sermon. *The key to interactive preaching is to amplify the text with the life context or symbolic levels of the listener, as mediated through the proclaimer.* That is the goal of the interactive questions— to reveal the various associations, personal and collective, "activated" in the lives of the listeners through the complex of the text. We will work out those questions shortly. Actually, these associations are there in every sermon, but normally we don't really know what they are. Nor do the listeners consciously know. Asking for that amplification in the sermon is a learning experience as people discover and remember experiences they never knew were so important to them, or were never associated with the text. My amplification as proclaimer, both at the life context level (my personal history with derelicts) and the symbolic level (exploring my own development and passages), is the opening to new aspects of attitudes and feelings.

Merely talking symbolically from the pulpit does not "access" symbolic material in the listener, even though it may appear so from these imperfect graphics. The opening, the penetration into different levels in the listener comes—if at all—from the interactive experience; i.e., in the interactive sermon, different levels are accessed through the invitation for an experience of those levels in a relational context. It is the relational experience that illumines the text in a way that historical and theological "amplifications" (sermon illustrations) usually fail to do, because the interactive questions ground the text in life experience. Again, the idea of a complex is helpful, because the text itself originally grew out of a life context (Jesus?) whose aspects can still be constellated in the complex of images within the text. By recovering the complex of images in the listeners, we are approximating the life context of the text. Thus the text becomes a complex, living experience.

Amplifying texts with personal and collective material is a helpful technique drawn from Jung. The second aspect of Jung's psychology that I find useful in interactive preaching is his typology by personality types. Most people are familiar with this typology through the Myers-Briggs Personality Type indicator. It was Jung who introduced the terms introversion and extraversion to our culture. He furthermore talked of four functions of the psyche: thinking and feeling as the two poles of making judgments, sensation and intuition as the two poles of making perceptions.

The most basic insight from Jung's typology is the recognition that persons do not make judgments or perceptions about life in the same way. In fact we all tend to lean to one side of the judgment (thinking or feeling) and perception (sensation or intuition) continuum, and exclude or undervalue the other side. Our personality type has a great deal to do with how each of us learns best, and how each of us responds to a sermon. Clearly none of the four functions is more valuable than any of the others. In fact, we cannot make our way through life without all four functions, even though—like the phenomenon of right- or left-handedness—it is difficult to use the functions that have been neglected and underdeveloped. However, it seems to me that the Protestant church has long valued thinking and sensation over feeling and intuition. The most important insight from this exploration of typology is that in our preaching we need to be aware of the different needs of different types.

A simpler way to talk about different personality types is found in Neuro Linguistic Programming (NLP). NLP is a school of therapy that grew out of observation of different types of therapists (Virginia Satir, Milton Erickson, and Fritz Perls, among others) actually doing therapy. The typology used in NLP corresponds to the three principle senses: vision, hearing, and feeling. NLP labels these types visuals, auditories, and kinesthetics. For instance, a visual might tend to use terms like "I see what you mean" or "We don't see eye to eye." A kinesthetic, however, might say "I've got a feel for that" or "I'm not grasping what you mean." And an auditory would choose the language, "I hear what you're saying" or "I really can't resonate with that."

If we think about a sermon from the point of view (as you can now *see*, throughout this book I have tended to use visual language) of the visual, kinesthetic, and auditory persons in the congregation, the traditional sermon is a primarily auditory event. The preacher stands in the pulpit and one listens. There is little movement, perhaps some facial expression seen from far away, so that the setting is not particularly a visual spectacle. From the kinesthetic point of view, a traditional sermon is likely to be "cold," because there's not a lot of movement, or touching, or interpersonal relating. Thus, a traditional sermon is likely to be an engaging experience for roughly one third of the congregation (auditories).

An interactive sermon, on the other hand, is an attempt to utilize all three representational systems *at the same time*. It is much more visually stimulating as the preacher moves much closer to the congregation and from place to place. As people respond to the sermon, there are more people to watch. Kinesthetics, naturally, will be the people in the congregation who are the most pleased with interactive preaching because there is so much movement, touching, and real emotion as an integral part of the sermon. Auditories might be the ones to miss the purely auditory experience of the traditional sermon read from the pulpit, but might find interactive preaching stimulating because they will have to listen very closely to who is speaking and will not be able to predict what will be said next. All in all, an interactive sermon is far more stimulating visually, kinesthetically, and audibly.

I have a friend who has been preaching interactively for a long time who tells me he has discovered that, after a period of interactive preaching, people begin to alter where they sit. The kinesthetics move right up to the front, wanting to be right in the middle of the action. The visuals sit in the middle where they are close enough to see what's happening, and the auditories sit in the back (where they probably sat in the first place) and quietly listen.

Another insight from the NLP typology is the notion of *accessing*.

In order for you to understand what I am saying to you, you have to take the words—which are nothing more than arbitrary labels for parts of your personal history—and *access* the meaning, namely some set of images, some set of feelings, or some set of sounds, which *are* the meaning for you of the word....That's a simple notion of how language works, and we call this process *transderivational search*. Words are triggers that tend to bring into your consciousness certain parts of your experience and not other parts.[10]

An interactive question asked in the context of a sermon may be thought of as a request for everyone in the congregation to *access* a piece of their personal history. Thus, how we ask the question—namely, which representational system we ask them to access—will in part determine whether they access the experience with images, feelings, or words, or even all three at the same time. For instance, in the sermon on the parable of the good Samaritan, if we want to ask people to make the connections to their own life context, they have to access those experiences before they can respond. NLP would predict that if we ask them to access those experiences kinesthetically, they would enter the memory at the feeling and sensation level. We might also presume that the kinesthetics in the congregation would be the ones most likely to enter into those feelings well enough to talk about them. The visuals and auditories would have some difficulty accessing the kinesthetic aspect of the memory. And likewise people might open another level of experience were we to ask them to access the memory visually or audibly. The language and phrasing of the question will, to a degree, determine the level of experience (images, feelings, words) we receive:

> Feeling access: "Can you *share* with us something about the *fears* experienced at a time when you were broken and wounded like the man on the road?"

> Image-oriented access: "What *images* come to mind when you *see* yourself during a time when you were broken and wounded like the man on the road?"

> Verbal access: "Can you *tell* us something about your *thoughts* at a time when you were broken and wounded like the man on the road?"

[10]Richard Bandler and John Grinder, *Frogs into Princes: Neuro Linguistic Programming.* Real People Press, 1979, p. 15.

Feeling/image/verbal access: "Can you see a picture in your mind, or remember what it felt like, or tell us about the things you thought about at a time when you were broken and wounded like the man on the road?"

Each of those questions will access the same memory in different ways. In preaching on the good Samaritan I particularly wanted the feeling experience, so I asked the question in a kinesthetic reference system. I have found it helpful, as the final part of preparing an interactive sermon, to review each question with a view to the representational system I want to access during the sermon. If I want people to see images, I use visual language. If I want the access to be at a feeling level, I use kinesthetic language. If I want people to discuss attitudes, I use auditory references. This approach works well with most types of interactive questions, except in the "symbolic exploration style" of sermon (discussed in chapter four). In symbolic exploration we ask people to experience biblical characters as inner figures, so the language is usually visual. In general, because of the nature of the interactive sermon, using primary language (visual images) and relational experience (feeling oriented), I find most of the questions should be phrased in visual and kinesthetic terms.

The direction of the above questions is toward the symbolic level of the text and the life context of the listener, probably coming out of my own life context as a proclaimer. This is done by asking people to access their experience as one in need. We could constellate a different field by shifting the questions. We could shift to the historical level of the text and direct the questions to a more symbolic level in the listener:

Feeling access: "Can you *share* something about the part of yourself you *fear* as your own worst enemy, like the Samaritan?"

Image-oriented access: "What do you *see* as your own worst enemy, like the Samaritan, in yourself?"

Verbal access: "Can you *say* something about the *attitudes* in yourself that are your own worst enemy, like the Samaritan?"

Feeling/image/verbal access: "Can you open (neutral term) the place in yourself that is your own worst enemy, like the Samaritan? What it feels like, or looks like, or sounds like?

Thus, the notion of *accessing* different levels of experience gives us a way to introduce new levels of experience into the sermon. NLP's reminder that different people access experience in different ways challenges us to rethink our entire approach to the worship experience.

A third school of psychological thought has also been informative. For many years, psychotherapy was oriented to the individual. Diagnostic terminology and treatment approaches were conceived as ways of thinking about and helping individual issues. Some therapists, however, began to notice that the ways in which couples and families got themselves into relational trouble could not be explained simply as the conglomeration of individual difficulties. Families could also be viewed as a system.

Systems thought tries to understand the behavior of individuals in families as the movement of interlocking and interdependent units of a self-contained system. The movement of one part of the system is never viewed in isolation, but as a movement that was effected by and will effect other parts of the system. A family system is a *holon*, as Salvador Minuchin and H. Charles Fishman use the term: both a part and a whole, both a self and a self-in-context.

This point of view changes the focus of therapy considerably. The therapist learns to pay attention to the context of interactions, rather than an isolated interaction in itself. The therapist learns to grasp the logic of the system rather than the pathology of the individual. For instance:

Different contexts call forth different facets....As a result people are always functioning with a portion of their possibilities. There are many possibilities, only some of which are elicited or constrained by the contextual structure. Therefore, breaking or expanding contexts can allow new possibilities to emerge. The therapist, an expander of contexts, creates a context in which exploration of the unfamiliar is possible. She confirms family members and encourages them to experiment with behavior that has previously been constrained by the family system. As new possibilities emerge, the family organism becomes more complex and develops more acceptable alternatives for problem solving.[11]

The church is a family system, and an interactive sermon can be thought of as a therapeutic intervention. The preacher, then, becomes the expander of contexts, and the sermon a creation of a context in which exploration of the unfamiliar is possible. The result of this sermonic intervention can be both new possibilities for individuals and new structures for the church family.

Think for just a moment of the traditional sermon from the pulpit as a family ritual within the system. It seems to me that the most adequate family parallel would be seeing the minister as the unassailable parent, secure in his or her authority within the family, instructing the family in the life commandments of just how to be a family. The congregation functions in this system as passive, dependent children, unable directly to confront the parent, and not valued for any input into the family discussion. The system works (achieves a "homeostasis") as long as the children feel nurtured and protected by the all-knowing parent. That is the proper role of parents with children at a certain age. However, the system will experience a great deal of stress in a situation where the children need to experiment with autonomy and initiative. What usually happens is some form of "acting out."

[11]Salvador Minuchin and H. Charles Fishman, *Family Therapy Techniques*. Harvard University Press, 1981, p. 15f.

Think for a minute now on the change introduced in the system when the minister leaves the pulpit and invites response. Suddenly the congregation is expected to take initiative and responsibility in the family meeting, rather than remaining passive and dependent. By moving to the same level as the congregation, the minister has crossed the boundary from the parental subsystem to the sibling subsystem. A new structure is called for, in which minister and congregation are now joint members of a common holon. Within that new structure the minister and congregation are confronted with new alignments of authority, responsibility, and boundaries. I am reminded of the difference in the nature of the interaction when I stand to the side and explain to my son how to keep his sandbox clean, and those other times when he instructs his baby sister on how to play with sand.

These reflections on a systemic way of thinking about sermons are no more than suggestions on the many parallels between church and family, sermons and therapy. Obviously, those parallels are too many and too important to overlook. For now, I simply want to emphasize the importance of physically moving out of the pulpit, and the healing possibilities that derive from that simple, but difficult, first step.

I do want to explore two important techniques in family therapy that I believe every interactive preacher needs to keep in mind. The paradoxical (or strategic) therapists call the first technique the principle of *positive connotation*. The principle of positive connotation is simply that the therapist in family therapy describes behavior in positive terms, rather than in blaming, labeling, critical terms that are often characteristic of the way dysfunctional families describe themselves. For instance, if the therapist wants to talk about a teenager's acting out, rather than saying something like "Johnny obviously has trouble dealing with authority," which gives his behavior a negative connotation, the therapist might instead say "Johnny is to be commended for his explorations of his own autonomy." There is an enormous difference between talking about

Johnny's behavior in negative or in positive terms. Labeling Johnny as a problem sets up the expectation that Johnny will in fact be a problem. He will tend to behave as he is expected to behave. Most importantly, the impasse in the family that brings the family to therapy most often has to do with the rigid pattern of interpreting one another's action. Positive connotation gives old behavior new meanings. Finally, positive connotation avoids the most serious obstacle to successful family therapy, which to my mind is getting caught in the family's way of seeing the world. Failure to use a positive connotation of behavior inevitably puts the therapist in the position of siding with one group or other within the family. The possibilities for change within the system are defeated by negative descriptions that lock family members into old roles.

Positive connotation is obviously paradoxical. Certainly some behaviors are destructive of family life, and others are constructive. However, from a systemic point of view, all family behavior is holistically and relationally determined. Positive connotation is simply a linguistic device that reminds us of the overlapping interrelations of the family. It frees us from the *linguistic tyranny* that mistakenly insists that the way we talk about a behavior is the only way it can be understood:

> We act as if we are locked into a certain kind of reality because of our language....[We] emphasize the fact that language is linear rather than circular. Therefore we tend to define behavior in terms of simple cause-effect, rather than systemic-circular, processes. The interactive and transactive nature of living systems is thereby ignored. In addition language emphasizes the digital—good vs. bad, black vs. white, normal vs. abnormal. It also keeps us on the level of content. In short, language is poorly designed to help us talk about relationships.[12]

[12]Gerald R. Weeks and Luciano L'Abate, *Paradoxical Psychotherapy: Theory and Practice with Individuals, Couples, and Families*. Brunner/Mazel Publishers, 1982, p. 107.

If we understand what the minister says in the context of an interactive sermon as very much like what a family therapist might say in the course of a session, it is clear that positive connotation is essential to the interactive process. Throughout the sermon the minister will be in the situation of responding to the congregation. Some of the stories, memories, and experiences will be spoken of in critical, blaming, and labeling ways. In the context of worship, the minister must be adept at rephrasing those stories in positive ways. For instance, suppose that in our interactive sermon on the good Samaritan, in response to the question, "Can you share something about the fears experienced at a time when you were broken and wounded like the man on the road?" a woman responds with a story about how alone and abandoned by her husband she felt during a hospital stay. If the minister responds to the story in a way that completely agrees with the connotation she has given to the experience, not only does the minister alienate the husband but the woman will continue her reference to that painful experience in a blaming, angry way. However, if the minister gives the story a positive connotation, then the effects of siding against the husband are mitigated, and more importantly, the woman is invited to see her experience in a new way. A therapist might go on to explore those feelings about her husband, but in a sermon we only want to open up her life context. For instance, in preaching an interactive sermon, I might give a positive connotation of that experience: "So, you remember that difficult time during your hospital stay as a time when you were relying on your own resources and reaching for things inside you which you had not previously thought you were capable of, is that right?" The blaming mentality of the story is not in the long run helpful to her or to the relationship, but confronted with a positive connotation of self-reliance and newly discovered capacities, she can see the same old story in a new and healing way.

In general, when responding to the stories told from the congregation, the minister should give each story a positive connotation. It preserves the healing atmosphere of the sermon, and challenges people to "reframe" the old stories with new meanings.

Reframing is a second important technique for interactive preaching borrowed from family therapy. Positive connotation, as we have seen, is an attempt to help people see old behavior in new ways, and is thus a form of reframing. Thus, reframing might be defined as changing "the conceptual and/or emotional setting or viewpoint in relation to which a situation is experienced and to place it in another frame which fits the 'facts' of the same concrete situation especially well, or even better, and thereby change its entire meaning....In short the meaning attributed to the situation is changed."[13]

The technique is used to give old behavior new meaning. A classic kind of paradoxical reframing has to do with the so-called "identified patient." A family therapist might say of the alcoholic father of a troubled family, "It is clear to me that Father is doing something very important to the family in making himself utterly dependent and in need of constant care-taking." Several things happen in this reframing. The old behavior of an isolated problem (Father's drinking) is reframed as a family predicament. Also, Father's adult behavior is reframed as dependent. Another example might be the senior in high school who is suddenly in danger of flunking. Although his parents conceive of this behavior as a direct attack upon them, the therapist might say, "Johnny is showing just how much he loves this family (even at great cost to himself), by eliminating any possibility that he would ever have to leave." A behavior (flunking) which had previously only been understood as damaging to the family is reframed as loving.

Reframing need not be quite that paradoxical. It simply offers new ways of understanding and interpreting old situations. In fact, a lot of what brings people to therapy can be seen as a failure to integrate multiple meanings and interpretations of the events of everyday life. People get

[13]*Ibid.*, p. 104.

stuck in one way of seeing their world, one frame of reference that is often inadequate to new situations.

Reframing is an important concept for interactive preaching. It might well be said that all preaching is in some way an attempt to "reframe" the lives of the listeners in the context of the gospel story. But interactive preaching in particular calls up stories, images, and feelings from the life context of the listener that put the scriptural stories into an entirely new, yet appropriate, frame. However, in the midst of the relational experience, those stories, images, and feelings from the listener are also reframed by the scripture. For example, if we invite people to experience their own brokenness side by side with the compassion of the Samaritan enemy, new meaning is created out of the parable. A cancer patient is invited to hear in the midst of her vulnerability that help comes from the most unexpected places. A newly divorced man in the midst of his isolation is invited to experience that other people can respond in love if he allows his need to be seen. That is what interactive preaching sets out to do: *to reframe each story within the meaning of the other by laying out the scriptural story and the story of the listener side by side.*

At the deepest level, faith itself is perhaps a grand reframing, for it invites us to understand and interpret our own experience in ways we might not otherwise do. It seems to me that is the goal of the interpretation of scripture, and thus, of preaching: that we reframe how we understand our lives along the pattern of the scriptural stories.

Historical Grounding

Preaching has historically been thought of as an intensely personal and often isolated endeavor. The traditional model pictures the proclaimer engaged in solitary study, alone at the typewriter, relying on the personal gifts of reason, rhetoric, style, and personality. The sermon itself is safely hidden away until Sunday morning and no one knows what the proclaimer will say until the moment of the sermon. Most often, no one knows of the reaction to the sermon except in the small ways that people let us know that the sermon met with approval or disapproval, appropriation or disinterest. The sermon exists in the mind of the minister and the impact exists in the minds of the listeners. We are trained to prepare the sermon in isolation, deliver the sermon in isolation, and find what response we can in isolation.

But in actuality the sermon process is an intensely interactive and interpersonal one. In its proper setting, the sermon from the very beginning has been a relational experience grounded in the Christian community. The form and style that shape our individual ways of preaching are grounded in our relationships with past preachers in our own lives, with professors we loved and admired, in the concrete needs of the people we serve. The content of our preaching is shaped by our own interaction with the history of faith, dogma, theology, and scripture. Without our interaction in the community of faith, there would be no sermon.

Thus, I want to argue that the interactive nature of preaching has always been implicit in the history of the Christian community. Interactive preaching simply makes the relational experience explicit, visible, and intentional.

However, a search through the history of preaching reveals few parallels to interactive preaching, even if those few are quite important. Already in the second century, theology began moving away from the more Eastern oral traditions of story, metaphor, and parable to forms of Greek Aristotelian logic. I find it interesting that the more Socratic style of reasoning was picked up in some ways by the Gnostics and other early heresies. As Christianity moved from the Hebrew world into the Roman world, preaching was influenced by Roman canons of rhetoric and oratory, rather than the more interactive rabbinic methods. Thus, from very early on, the content of preaching was shaped by rational modes of thought, and the form of preaching was shaped by the devices of rhetoric.

A sociological analysis of the history of preaching yields some interesting insights into interactive preaching. The first has to do with the relationship between style and culture. Preaching has always borrowed its style from culture. For instance, during the scholastic period preaching was full of allegory, stories of the saints, and the famous four-fold interpretation, all of which reflected the medieval world view of the three-tiered universe and the manifold structure of God. Preaching style in the baroque period was as flowery and ornamental as baroque architecture. The Enlightenment brought rational, highly philosophical and doctrinal preaching to the forefront, while the Romantic era saw an emphasis on emotion and nature. *Preaching style follows culture*. It should not be surprising, then, that in our age interactive preaching should develop as a style that focuses primarily on the relational and interpersonal. Our age is the age of the relationship as no other age has been before it. Interactive preaching is simply the same kind of expression of the style of an age as have been other preaching styles in other ages.

The second insight has to do with the recognition that the history of preaching has most often been written by educated, influential men in seminaries and the church. The sermons on which their histories were based have tended to be the sermons of educated, influential men through history whose sermons were most likely to be recorded and preserved.

However, preaching right along side of the educated and influential were those preachers who were uneducated and powerless. Their sermons were just as stylish but in different ways, and just as needed by their own struggling people as the sermons that history has remembered. Only quite recently have historians begun to note the preaching of women, blacks, campesinos, native Americans, and others. For the most part, their preaching has been overlooked, and interactive preaching has been a piece of that history. Excluded from traditional education and from the halls of power, they drew their style from the people around them.

This leads us to the third consideration: The style of preaching is directly related to the sociology of preaching.

Learned oratory and stylish rhetoric are characteristic of
one level of social life; participation and dialogue are
characteristic of another. Parallels to interactive preaching—whether it be "free prayer," responses, or lay participation—can be cited among Quakers, Moravians, Seventh
Day Adventists, Jehovah's Witnesses, Pentecostals, Holi-
ness churches, Black Baptists, and the African Methodist
Episcopal church, among others.[14] What I find most interesting about the similarities in all of these groups, is the
fact that at one time or another each of these groups has
been ostracized, persecuted, or otherwise excluded from
participation in the mainstream of Protestant religious
life. That status as oppressed, persecuted, or powerless
people has left its mark on the style of preaching.

Thus, interactive preaching is in many ways liberation
preaching. Paulo Freire gives us a challenging picture of
the oppressed in his book, *Pedagogy of the Oppressed*. He
points out that one of the most difficult tasks in liberating
the oppressed lies not only with the outer facts of oppres-
sion, but with the inner results. Thus Freire proposes a
pedagogy of "problem-solving education" which aims not
at "teaching" problem solving, but at *conscientization*, that
is, education in which consciousness of the historical
situation, limitations, and possibilities within themselves
are spoken by the oppressed, rather than as a program, or
world view, supplied by the "benevolent" teacher.
Conscientization, a way of claiming their world and their
ideas for their own, is Freire's goal. The only way he sees
to accomplish this purpose is an education based on dialogue.

Liberating education consists in acts of cognition,
not transferrals of information. It is a learning
situation in which the cognizable object (far from
being the end of the cognitive act) intermediates

[14]See *The Westminster Dictionary of Worship*, edited by J. G.
Davies, articles on worship in various religious traditions. Westminster
Press, 1971.

the cognitive actors—teacher on the one hand and students on the other....Dialogical relations—indispensable to the capacity of the cognitive actors to cooperate in perceiving the same cognizable object—are otherwise impossible.

Indeed, problem-posing education, which breaks with the vertical patterns characteristic of banking education, can fulfill its function of freedom only if it can overcome the above contradiction. Through dialogue, the teacher-of-the-students and the students-of-the-teacher cease to exist and a new term emerges: teacher-students with student-teachers. The teacher is no longer merely the one who teaches, but is one who is...taught in the dialogue with the students, who in turn while being taught also teach. They become jointly responsible for a process in which all grow. In this process, arguments based on "authority" are no longer valid; in order to function, authority must be *on the side of* freedom, not *against* it. Here, no one teaches another, nor is anyone self-taught. [They] teach each other, mediated by the world.[15]

We only need to substitute the word *preach* where Freire uses the word *teach* in order to understand the liberating nature of interactive, dialogical preaching. I want to suggest that forerunners of interactive preaching are found in religious groups that were at one time—or continue to be—oppressed, persecuted, or otherwise ostracized precisely on the basis that Freire points out: Conscientization of oppressed people requires a pedagogy *and a homiletic* based on dialogue. Obviously, some of these groups have continued to teach and preach in the style of the dominant culture, while others moved to a more interactive model. I am suggesting simply that historical occurrences of dialogical preaching styles between preach-

---

[15]Paulo Freire, *Pedagogy of the Oppressed*. Herder and Herder, 1971, p. 67.

ers and congregations who address one another as equals are directly related to their experience of being cast out of more hierarchically structured social groups. Finding themselves socially equalized, some of these groups moved to keep themselves liturgically equalized. The dialogical model, as Freire reminds us, is uniquely suited for communication between people who meet one another on the same level.

What is the alternative to the dialogical model? Freire describes what he calls the "banking concept" of education in which "education thus becomes an act of depositing, in which students are the depositories and the teacher is the depositor."[16] Again, I suggest we need only to substitute the word *preach* where Freire uses the word *teach* to understand the implications of the promise of the interactive style among oppressed groups, because the "banking concept" of education and homiletics "maintains and even stimulates the contradiction" between teacher and student.[17] Using his model, I offer this parallel as the "banking concept of homiletics":

(a) The preacher preaches and the listeners are preached at.
(b) The preacher knows everything and the listeners know nothing.
(c) The preacher thinks and the listeners are thought about.
(d) The preacher disciplines and the listeners are disciplined.
(e) The preacher chooses and enforces his choice, and the listeners comply.
(f) The preacher acts and the listeners have the illusion of acting through the action of the preacher.
(g) The preacher chooses the sermon content, and the listeners (who are not consulted) adapt to it.

[16]*Ibid.*, p. 58.
[17]*Ibid.*, p. 59.

(h) The preacher confuses the authority of knowledge with professional authority, which sets the preacher in opposition to the freedom of the listeners.
(i) The preacher is the subject of the learning process, while the listeners are mere objects.

Dialogue between valued equals, without teachers and students, without preachers and listeners, was an alternative open to a variety of religious outcasts through history. Among the historical parallels that I could cite for interactive preaching, I want to focus on three primary examples: black preaching, Quaker worship, and the testimony.

Black preaching has always been relational preaching. The responsive and participational atmosphere of worship has deep roots in black culture. "The all-consuming, passionate abandon so characteristic of black culture worship has no doubt been an escape from brutal reality and a survival technique."[18]

The Black style, which includes a pattern of call-and-response, is very easily traceable to Black African culture. Such response requires a participating audience. Black preaching has had such an audience from the beginning. It has been shaped by interaction with that audience—hammered out in dialogue with Black brothers and sisters. If the Black preaching style is unique, then that uniqueness depends in part upon the uniqueness of the Black congregation which talks back to the preacher as a normal part of the pattern of worship....In the participatory response of their congregations Black preachers have a rare resource which needs greater understanding and appreciation.[19]

Thus black preaching has always been a relational experience in worship. Preaching in this context is far

---

[18]Henry H. Mitchell, *Black Preaching*. J.B. Lippincott Co., 1970, p. 34.
[19]*Ibid.*, p. 95f.

61

removed from academic style, although black congregations tend to value education, denied to so many of them,
far more than white congregations. Rather, preaching is
an exposition of a shared truth, a shared story, lived out in
the lives of the people in the congregation. Both the
proclaimer and the people share in telling the story.

If we think historically about the black church experience, it is important to remember that the first black
preachers were chosen from their own congregations. They
were not outsiders. They shared not only a common faith
but a common life experience, working side by side with
their people during the week and preaching on Sundays.
This "intimacy" is a far cry from a concept of ministry in
which the one who proclaims is entirely set apart from the
congregation—a different education, a different lifestyle,
and perhaps even a different faith language. Thus the
shared identity and intimacy of a proclaimer called from
within the community forms a basis for interaction. The
rapport between the proclaimer and the congregation
necessarily alters the relational pattern. Listeners in the
black church feel they are being addressed *personally* and
so they respond to the friend who addresses them. They
respond in relationship.

In fact I think it is possible to say the experience of the
black church is based on an entirely different understanding of *community*. Whereas so often in traditional preaching, the role of the person in the pulpit is that of translator,
bridging the language barrier between the contemporary
congregation and the ancient scripture, the role of the
black preacher is "the stimulator or initiator of the dialogue."[20] In essence, a translator speaks from outside the
life context of the congregation (subject-object dualism
maintained), while the black minister speaks in the midst
of the life context of the congregation (subject-object dualism overcome). In others words, the operative function of
community is radically different. For the translator in the

[20]*Ibid.*, p. 110.

pulpit, the community is the larger Christian community, the historical identity of the church, into which the listener must be brought weekly. The community re-forms, re-gathers in every worship service. Historically, for the black proclaimer, the community was already defined and no translation was necessary. There was already a defining experience, the experience of being black and oppressed. There was already a relatedness that could be the basis of interactive preaching.

There is a different nature of community when people live out of a defining experience. The sociology of preaching is shifting underneath our feet. Given the transient movement of our culture, with so many of us moving from state to state as we move through the life cycle, congregations are more and more likely to be gatherings of pilgrim strangers. Furthermore, as denominational preferences fall away, congregations are less likely to be theologically homogenous. We are preaching in congregations without defining experiences. We are preaching in congregations struggling to find community. Yet all too often the language of our preaching assumes the listeners share a common identity. We preach in the first person plural— "We are the body of Christ," "We are one in the Spirit"—but without a defining experience there is no "we." A congregation may be theologically the body of Christ, but without being grounded in a shared experience it may operatively remain a people seeking definition. The black church reminds us of what it can mean to be a community of shared experience. Interactive preaching, moving away from the language of "we" to the dialogical language of "you" and "I," can become the defining experience that forms a community.

There are three other insights from the black tradition in which I find helpful parallels to interactive preaching. The content of black preaching historically has tended to be grounded in a "felt need" of the community, rather than in doctrinal or intellectual issues. A review of the sermons of Dr. Martin Luther King, Jr. finds remarkably little reference to debates among theories of atonement, historical intricacies of biblical texts, or current theological controversies, although he was a learned man. The content focuses squarely on vital issues in the life context of the people he was addressing.

Also, in terms of the form of the sermon, black preaching relies heavily on primary language. When Jesse Jackson preaches, one is immediately aware of being in the hands of a master storyteller. His rhetoric does not take the form of concepts, but of word-pictures. Story, metaphor, and symbol become the basic form of the sermon. Dr. Martin Luther King, Jr.'s "I Have a Dream" speech is a wonderful example of primary language: first person references, alliteration, word-pictures, symbolic allusions.

Finally, I want to point our that in terms of style, traditionally, black ministers do not launch immediately into the sermon. Rather, they begin the sermon process by "warming up" the audience, intentionally taking the time to create a relational atmosphere. This is as much an introduction to the person behind the pulpit as it is an introduction to the sermon. When the proper rapport is felt, then the sermon proper begins. This rapport is crucial, for it prepares the ground for what will happen next in the sermon. Interacting in a sermon is "risky" both for the persons responding and for the proclaimer, if it is to be "true dialogue." Only a healing atmosphere that is safe and accepting invites the dialogue. Something personal is ventured and shared in participation in the community. The risk involved is the risk of self-disclosure. As Mitchell points out, "In a hostile white world, they have had to be close-lipped and poker-faced to survive....And yet there must be some place where Blacks can actually open up and let feelings out safely. The Black church has been that place. The healing catharsis inherent in the Black worship service has enabled many generations of Blacks to keep their balance and sanity."[21] I would add only that all of us are too often "poker-faced" and need a space that invites a healing catharsis of our own.

[21]*Ibid.*, p. 110f.

Given the nature of the catharsis that is so characteristic of black worship, it is not surprising that the entire worship experience is dominated by a sense of unpredictability and openness. This openness to the movement of the Spirit is rooted in a trust that if hearts are open, God will be present in the experience. This trust in the nature of religious experience is the foundation of the interactive process in black worship. Interactive preaching is grounded in that same trust in the movement of the Spirit and in religious experience. It is simply a contemporary expression of the openness that black worship in America has celebrated for more than two hundred years.

There is another faith group that has historically grounded its worship experience in a complete openness to the movement of the Spirit. Quaker worship has from the beginning been a collective, communal experience of seeking openings into the "Inner Light." The Quaker revolution—and it was and continues to be a "revolution" (a turning)—has for more than three centuries challenged the traditional Protestant idea of what it means to be "church."

Although firmly rooted in Christianity, Quakerism has never had a fixed set of theological beliefs. Friends have generally felt that it is the reality of a person's religious experience that matters, not the symbols with which he tries to describe this experience. A direct experience of God is open to anyone who is willing to sit quietly and search diligently for it, Quakers believe. There are no prerequisites for this experience, neither the institution of the church, not its sacraments, nor a trained clergy, not even the message of the Bible, unless illuminated by the Inner Light. Every person has the capacity for religious experience, just as he has the capacity to fall in love, but he must be willing to approach worship with an open heart, experientially.[22]

[22]Margaret Hope Baker, *The Quiet Rebels: The Story of the Quakers in America*. New Society Publishers, 1985, p. 5f.

That openness and trust of religious experience, so deep in the heart of Quakerism, is a field of the fertile soil from which the idea of interactive preaching has grown. With that grounding in the experiential level of life, interactive preaching is essential. Without that grounding, finding the roots of our preaching in the secondary language of theology and dogma, interactive preaching is at best a technique. The same insistence on a return to the religious experience at the heart of Christian faith, present in interactive preaching, found earlier expression in the Quaker movement. It has also been found century after century.

Any uniqueness in Quaker religious thought is not to be found in its novelty, but rather in its recovery of something which is easily lost, the idea that true religion must be genuinely *experiential.* The God who is like Jesus Christ can indeed be inferred by argument, but that is never sufficient. It is experience, especially the experience of the changed life, that is the true verification. This is another way of saying that Quakers place strong emphasis on the doctrine of the Holy Spirit...reaching directly into the human heart, giving guidance and strength in life's darkest as well as life's brightest ways.[23]

The earliest Quakers met in homes or even in fields for their worship. The traditional worship service begins in a meditative silence without any preconditions. As foreign as it may seem in our noisy world, silence can be a creative silence when it becomes a discipline. This is the practice of Quaker worship. It requires a great discipline for every individual involved because often there is no specially trained or designated clergy person present. The silence

---

[23]D. Elton Trueblood, *The People Called the Quakers: The Enduring Influence of a Way of Life and a Way of Thought.* Harper & Row, 1966, p. 67.

may last for up to an hour until someone feels moved to speak. The words spoken may be a personal decision made in the previous week, a prayer offered, a hymn spontaneously sung, a scripture quoted from memory and offered for reflection. Quakers talk about having a sense of a "gathered" meeting in which the individual and unrehearsed moments coalesce to form a meaningful whole that speaks to everyone present.

The notion that Quaker worship is based on silence alone is inaccurate. The guiding principle of Quaker worship is openness to God, rather than a code of silence. The distinction is important. Some of the earliest Quakers, called the Seekers, had already—before they first met George Fox—gathered for worship without any commitment to silence or speech, but simply to gather, to listen, to wait, and to seek to be obedient. "To be obedient," says Trueblood, "is to be deeply engaged and consequently responsive. The person who is determined to say nothing and who thinks of himself merely as 'audience' has not begun to understand what the significance of obedience is."[24] So significant is the orientation toward obedience rather than silence that Quakers circulated the following simple instructions to a worship service as a part of the assembly of the World Council of Churches held in Amsterdam in 1948:

> WORSHIP, according to the ancient practice of the Religious Society of Friends, is entirely without human direction or supervision. A group of devout persons come together and sit down quietly with no prearrangement, each seeking to have an immediate sense of divine leading and to know first hand the presence of the Living Christ. It is not wholly accurate to say that such a Meeting is held on the basis of Silence; it is more accurate to say that it is held on the basis of "Holy Obedience." Those who enter such a Meeting can harm it in two specific

[24]*Ibid.*, p. 88.

ways: first, by an advance determination to speak; and second, by advance determination to keep silent. The only way in which a worshipper can help such a Meeting is by an advance determination to try to be responsive in listening to the still small voice and doing whatever may be commanded. Such a Meeting is always a high venture in Faith and it is to this venture we invite you this hour.

It is important to note that many, if not most, contemporary Quakers do not meet for worship according to the old style every single Sunday. Quaker worship today, like the Quaker faith, is a picture of diversity and contrasts. This diversity in worship is itself a testimony to the openness to all varieties of religious experience and expression found among Quakers. It is also important to note that the traditional Quaker worship has not failed to produce great preachers, men and women. In fact, virtually all of the earliest Quakers preached wherever they went to whoever would listen in whatever setting could be found.

However, the depth of the Quaker testimony is a silent depth—to preach without words. Although it must be noted that silence in not the rule, as is generally thought of Quakers, seeking God in the stillness remains the primary orientation of Quaker worship. Interactive preaching can learn a great deal from the Quaker experience of silence, because the healing, reflective atmosphere of worship that silence creates is essential for opening up a relational experience during the sermon.

The very discipline of getting one's body still and one's mind still, dismissing the multitude of worries and concerns, is often highly beneficent, and the best of it is that such a process does not require any special talent or aptitude....It is not sufficient, for creative silence, merely to abstain from words. We must also...abstain at times from all of our thoughts, imaginations, and desires. The result can be a "flood of refreshment." There is a sense in which those who seek are likely to find, but there is

68

another, equally important sense, in which those
who seek, especially if they seek frantically, are
hindered from finding....The encounter with the
Living God often comes best when we cease to try
and are simply willing to wait....The silence which
modern man needs, especially in view of the ca-
cophony of radio and television, is not the mere
outward silence of the lips, but a deep silence of
mind and heart.[25]

The Quakers teach us that if we are going to learn to
preach from experience, even preach in the midst of experience, we have to learn how to preach without talking all
the time.

The third and final piece of history that I would like to
review in connection with interactive preaching is the
practice of giving a "testimony." Most of us who were raised
in any sort of evangelical-style church are familiar with
the practice. At a Sunday evening service, or church camp,
or maybe during a revival, the preacher at one point or
another would call for someone to give a testimony. That
person would usually stand, face the congregation, and tell
the story of how God had changed her life, or just what a
sinner he was before he found Jesus, or the circumstances
of her own conversion. Sometimes they stammer, not
really sure how to put the story together. Sometimes they
mumble inaudibly. At other times someone would shout
and cry and really "lose it," so that an elder or a deacon
might have to take a few minutes with them while the
service went on. Of course, in many Baptist, Pentecostal,
or Church of God congregations today, the practice of
giving a testimony is still strong.

"Testimony" has its roots in the revivals of the First
and Second Great Awakenings. It is the stuff of open-air
preaching and the camp meetings. "Testimony" comes
from the same Greek word that gives us our English word
"martyr," and in that sense the greatest testimony a

[25]*Ibid.*, p. 94.

person could give was the gift of his or her own life. Historically, the first hint of the practice of a layperson recounting a story from their life history at the invitation of the preacher is found in the open-air preaching of George Whitefield (1714-1770) in England and America. Whitefield came into contact with the Wesley brothers at Oxford. Ordained a deacon in the Church of England, at the Wesley's urging he took off for Georgia. Upon his return to England he was ordained a priest, "but the clergy looked upon him with distrust as an enthusiast, and he was not invited to preach in the churches."[26] Excluded from the pulpits, he took up open-air preaching (February, 1739). This consisted of finding an available field, erecting some primitive sort of podium, publicizing a meeting with any sort of media available, and preaching to all who came. Very soon he was preaching to crowds larger than could have been placed inside a church building. He invited John Wesley to join him, and on April 2, 1739, John Wesley preached to a crowd of about three thousand, going to preach often in such open-air pulpits.

That is the story of how the sermon got moved from a pulpit in a church to a podium in a field. And the sermon has never really been the same since. George Whitefield heard of one John Newton, who had at one time been a sea captain in the slave trade. Upon hearing the story of Newton's conversion and subsequent reform, Whitefield invited Newton to tell the story at one of his open-air meetings. John Newton, of course, went on to become a minister himself, worked very hard to end slavery in Britain, and is best remembered as the hymnodist who wrote "Amazing Grace."

Thus the practice of a layperson giving a testimony probably has its roots in the responses people made to revivalist preaching, shared with the preacher, and were later asked to share with the audience. It is a personalized *Heilsgeschichte* (sacred history). The testimony arises from

[26]Edwin Charles Dargan, *A History of Preaching, Volume II*. Baker Book House, 1954, p. 311.

the need to reflect on religious experience, not at a secondary, technical level but really as a way of owning the experience by reliving it as a story.

There are two kinds of stories that are especially important as vehicles for religious expression. The first is *autobiography*, or "testimony," the first person account of the teller's struggle with the gods and demons. It begins inside the speaker and says, "This is what happened to me." Recently neglected, testimony deserves reinstatement as a primary mode of religious discourse. It is a genre which celebrates the unique, the eccentric and the concrete. I suspect its decline in recent years is related to our industrial society's emphasis on interchangeable units, both human and mechanical, and its consequent suspicion of the particular and the irregular. But that is just what is valuable about autobiography. It reclaims personal uniqueness in an era of interchangeability. In an age of externality it uncovers what the classic mystics once described as "interiority." Autobiography is *my* story.[27]

Testimony is autobiography. Seen in that way, testimony becomes a way of self-understanding, as well as communal sharing. Only by telling the story do we truly know ourselves. Thus, the testimony serves as a vehicle not only for self-disclosure but ultimately for self-understanding.

The self expresses itself by the metaphors it creates and projects, and we know it by those metaphors; *but it does not exist as it now does and as it now is before creating its metaphors.* We do not see or touch the self, but we do see and touch its metaphors: and thus we "know" the self, activity or

[27]Harvey Cox, *The Seduction of the Spirit: The Use and Misuse of People's Religion.* Simon and Schuster, 1973, p. 9.

agent, represented in the metaphor and the metaphorizing.[28]

There is a sense in which we do not really know ourselves until we begin to see our life as a story. Otherwise life is just a series of random, unrelated experiences and relationships. It is not until we construct the story, the metaphor, the personal "myth," of our own life that we begin to see it more as a whole. Giving our "testimony" is thus a way to form our experience into a story that gives our life meaning.

[Autobiography] makes it possible for all the events and relationships of our life to show us what they were *for*, what their purpose was in our lives, and what they wish to tell us for the future. Thus we gradually discover that our life has been going somewhere, however blind to its direction and however unhelpful to it we ourselves may have been. We find that a connective thread has been forming beneath the surface of our lives, carrying the meaning that has been trying to establish itself in our existence. As we recognize and identify with it, we see an inner myth that has been guiding our lives unknown to ourselves.[29]

I do not want to claim too much for the testimony. Clearly, it is subject to abuses, just as are the Quaker silence and the response of the black congregation. Over time, giving a testimony may be reduced to giving an expected rendition in traditional form of one or another amazing experiences that might be entertaining or boring. Yet we cannot overlook the fact that the testimony represents one of the few historical experiences of people "theologizing" or preaching in the first person. This is precisely

[28]James Olney, *Metaphors of the Self: The Meaning of Autobiography*. Princeton University Press, 1972, p. 34.
[29]Ira Progoff, *At a Journal Workshop*. Dialogue House Library, 1975, p. 11.

the aim of interactive preaching. Asking for a testimony invites people to do something remarkable: speak the gospel from the center of their own life context and experience. Testimony is as simple and as difficult as John Newton's being able to say, "I once was lost, but now am found; was blind, but now I see."

Testimony means the telling and retelling of my story. This is not a merely marginal human need. Some psychologists believe it is an utterly central one. If people cannot tell and retell their story, they go mad....Testimony goes beyond both silence and system....Testimony is me telling my story in a world of people with stories to tell. It is an effort to construct a common world that fuses authentic interiority with genuine community. Mostly the attempt fails, or at least does not succeed completely. But we never stop trying.[30]

---

[30]Harvey Cox, *The Seduction of the Spirit*, p. 96f.

PREPARING TO PREACH INTERACTIVELY

Preparing the Congregation

In this chapter I want to lay out some suggestions for beginning to preach interactively. Given the nature of interactive preaching, a different sort of preparation is called for than with most other styles of sermons. To give this interactive process the best chance of being accepted and useful to the congregations we work with, we need to give thought to a variety of issues before simply walking out of the pulpit and asking for responses.

Those of us coming out of traditions in which response to the sermon in the context of worship is totally unknown will have to prepare the congregation for this new experience. As with most new ideas, it seems essential to run the idea through the normal channels of congregational life. The first step might be for the minister to present the idea of a "trial period" of perhaps an interactive sermon series (three or four consecutive sermons) to the governing body of the congregation (church board, worship committee, etc.), explaining the purpose and value of the interactive process. Following another route, perhaps a study committee could be created to study the interactive sermon process and then bring the idea forward. The goal of the preparation is to spread the ownership of the interactive

73

sermon process out to as many people as possible. The more people who are a part of the process and have input into the decisions, the less likely interactive preaching will meet with resistance. The idea of a trial period gives folks the comfort of knowing that anything can be endured for a period of time and that they will have a chance to respond after the experience. Of course, following the initial experiment, the minister should go back to the governing body for responses and suggestions. If all goes well, it might be helpful to have some sort of statement of approval for the interactive process in the future.

From the very beginning it needs to be made clear that the interactive sermon will not replace other styles of preaching. In my own experience, I have found it best to preach interactively only sparingly when the style is first introduced (usually in a series of two or three sermons), and later, with full approval of the congregation, no more than half of the time.

Another avenue of broadening the support for interactive preaching within a congregation is the use of whatever media are available. The church newsletter can be a valuable tool for helping everyone know more about just what to expect from an interactive sermon. I could see the church newsletter being used to describe an interactive sermon, cite historical parallels, talk about autobiography, primary language, the priesthood of all believers, etc. It seems important that the congregation be told in advance of the first interactive sermon what will be expected of them (i.e., they will simply be given the opportunity to respond to a question), and the rationale for preaching in the interactive style rather than a more traditional style. A response in the newsletter from the minister following the first sermon, thanking people for their participation, also would be helpful. The worship bulletin can also be quite helpful as a place to give some brief definition or description of an interactive sermon and a written invitation for participation (which might help visitors figure out why people are talking back to the preacher). I have found it helpful to always list the sermon in the bulletin as

"Interactive Sermon," followed by the title, thus giving folks a chance, when glancing through the bulletin, to prepare for responses. This turned out to be particularly important for the choir, who wanted to determine before the service where they would sit for an interactive sermon.

Another level of preparation has to do with the style of worship in a particular congregation. Interactive preaching is from the beginning a commitment to a more relational, more participatory—some might say, more informal—style of worship. An interactive sermon in the midst of a worship service that is otherwise completely passive is a contradiction. There need to be ways to begin a gradual movement toward a relational and participatory style of worship. Lay participation is crucial. The more experience and commitment lay people have in taking part in worship (reading, praying, preaching), the more likely they are to value the interactive process. Experiences such as an informal period of greeting (from time to time), rather than an organ prelude, begin the process of people relating to one another in the context of worship. I have also found it helpful to print the scripture readings for the morning in the bulletin (if pew Bibles are not available), and invite the congregation to read particularly important or well-known passages aloud with me. One of the most helpful movements toward a more relational style of worship is to present the pastoral prayer from the floor with the congregation, rather than from the pulpit. People in my congregation found it quite helpful for me to ask for any prayer concerns. People would usually stand and mention a name and a situation, to which I would refer specifically in the prayer. We also found it helpful to have written prayer request forms which were collected before the pastoral prayer. Such a form of pastoral prayer is quite interactive and prepares the ground for interactive preaching. I suggest that all of these elements toward a more relationally oriented worship be in place before experimenting with interactive preaching.

A good deal of thought needs to be given to the first interactive sermon preached in a congregation. It may be the first experience anyone (including the preacher) has had with the interactive style. In addition to the preparations in the newsletter, bulletin, and others mentioned previously, something needs to be said in the sermon itself. I usually begin a first sermon in that style with some sort of acknowledgment of how uncomfortable or unusual it might feel for myself and the congregation to be in that situation, face to face. Then I think it is important to explicitly express real interest in the responses the congregation will make, affirming that their testimony, thoughts, feelings, and life experiences are a crucial arena for theology—that what they have to say is very important for all to hear. I usually conclude such an introduction with a reference to Jesus' preaching, which was not from the pulpit and was often interactive. Such an opening statement might say something like this:

This is going to be a different kind of sermon series. For a number of reasons, probably it will be one of the most complicated series of sermons I've preached. First of all, the style of preaching during this series is going to be different. I call this style "interactive preaching." For the next three weeks I'll be out of the pulpit during the sermon and interact a great deal more with you. (Does it feel a little uncomfortable to you to have me out here? Feels a little unusual to me too.) This puts us face to face, without the pulpit to keep me safe. It is going to be more difficult for me, and probably for you. This kind of interaction in a sermon doesn't come naturally to us. For me it will require that I preach a little more from the heart than from the head; more from an outline than from a prepared text as I usually preach. So it's going to stretch me as a person and as a preacher. I believe it will stretch you as well. And that's fine. We could all use a little stretching.

Interactive preaching is participatory. You'll have a chance, which I hope you'll use, to participate in being a preacher, a co-proclaimer, with me. In each of these sermons I'll ask at least two questions that I want several of you actually to speak up and talk about in your own words. I want to say that the way you see things, what you have to say, your feelings, your stories from your own experience, are just as important as anything I might say from the pulpit.

My goal in preaching this way is simply to see if interactive preaching doesn't generate more energy in worship, a more experiential quality to worship. I imagine it being something more like Jesus' sermons must have been. He didn't preach from a pulpit and his followers didn't listen in comfortable pew benches. Instead they were sometimes out in the open, sitting together in a circle, close to each other. Jesus talked, asked questions, listened as others spoke and asked him questions. I hope this method of preaching can be something like that and a growing experience for all of us.

In the sermons that follow in this series I will usually begin each with a similar introduction in order to sort of bring folks back into the moment, and also to help those who missed the previous sermon feel included in what's going on.

Beginning to preach interactively also requires some thinking about the style and extent of the interaction requested. In the following chapter, I will lay out four styles of interactive preaching, beginning with what I see as the most basic and moving toward the more difficult. For instance, the first sermon out of the pulpit might well be a directed question sermon, since these sermons ease into the interactive process with two to five interactive questions. A little later, the shared storytelling sermon is a natural interactive setting. The two most difficult styles, symbolic exploration and parabling, I leave until the congregation is quite comfortable with the interactive style. Then I can preach from any of the types as best fits the sermon material for that week.

Preparing the Proclaimer

Preparing ourselves to preach interactively is a more subtle, but perhaps a more difficult, task than preparing the congregation. For in preparing ourselves we face our own preconceptions, our own limitations, our own issues.

Using the model we constructed in chapter two, remember that one way to think about the psychology of a sermon involves the field constellated by the interaction of the various levels of the proclaimer, the listener, and the text. In many ways, we could say *the different levels of the text engage different levels of the listener as mediated through the proclaimer*. In other words, if we want to engage other levels in the listener, we first have to engage other levels in ourselves.

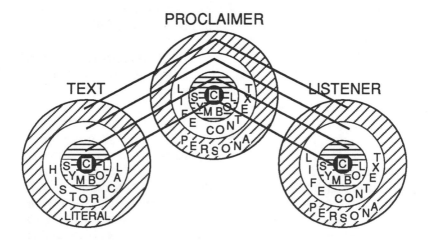

Ministers encounter people at the persona level every day. By the persona of the minister, I simply mean the built-in patterns of relating to a "minister" that all of us have within us. Experience teaches us typical patterns of relating to certain classes of persons such as doctors, teachers, presidents, and ministers. More often than not, our relationships with these "personae" are more determined by precisely those inner models than by the outer reality of the person in the role. For instance, on the authority of that inner image we respond without question to the doctor's request that we take off our clothes, while in other settings such a request would be highly inappropriate. Similarly we allow dentists to manipulate our mouths, hairstylists to massage our heads, police officers to frisk our bodies—all of these being intrusions into deeply personal space. We allow these intrusions on the strength of the persona rather than on an intimacy with the person behind the role.

I suggest that the "authority" of the minister is directly related to the persona. The different aspects of the persona reveal the different aspects of authority. Interactive preaching forces us to reexamine the relationship between preaching and authority and, thereby, both the understanding of the nature of preaching and the value we ascribe to it. I invite every would-be interactive preacher to examine his or her typical patterns of confronting roles, values, and trust as the first step in moving beyond the persona. A minister, for instance, has the authority of the position, the authority of the office, as in the original meaning of the term "aristocrat." Also, the minister has the authority of knowledge, a kind of theological "technocrat." Finally, the minister also has the authority of entrance into people's lives in difficult situations, the one who goes among the people, as in the root meaning of "democrat" (*demos*, the people).

From which aspect of the role does the sermon derive its authority—aristocrat, technocrat, or democrat? My sense is that traditionally the authority of the sermon is grounded in the aristocratic and technocratic aspects of the role, more akin to the authority of the chairman of the board and the scholar, than to the relational authority of the one among the people. In preparing to preach interactively, all of us need to give some careful reflection to how we wear the role (the persona mask) of minister, for the interactive sermon clearly aims to speak out of the experience of being "of the people," the reality of being a person in a life context as well as a persona. That is its authority—relational authority. The chairman of the board speaks out of the experience of the institution, while the scholar speaks out of the experience of history. Interactive preaching challenges us to speak out of a different level of our authority as ministers.

The first step beyond the persona level raises the question of value: not only *what* we value as ministers, but *how* we value. There are two different ways of valuing on a continuum from the superlogical to the intimately related, from the formal and abstract to the contextual and narrative, from rights and rules to responsibilities and relationships, from the logic of justice to the ethics of care. Many of us (especially men) learn to make decisions about what is important to us on a hierarchy of values: Above is better than below, larger is better than smaller, more is better than less. Value decisions are based upon where the values fall in the hierachy of justice. Others of us (mostly women) have learned to make decisions about what is important to us through a web of relationships: Intimacy is better than isolation, caring is better than strength, human contact is more essential than logic. These two images, the hierarchy and the web, express two different ways of valuing.

The images of hierarchy and web, drawn from the texts of men's and women's fantasies and thoughts, convey different ways of structuring relationships and are associated with different views of morality and self....Thus the images of hierarchy and web inform different modes of assertion and response: the wish to be alone at the top and the subsequent fear that others will get too close; the wish to be at the center of connection and the consequent fear of being too far out on the edge. These disparate fears of being stranded and being caught give rise to different portrayals of achievement and affiliation, leading to different modes of action and different ways of assessing the consequences of choice.

...These disparate visions in their tension reflect the paradoxical truths of human experience—that we know ourselves as separate only insofar as we live in connection with others, and that we experience relationship only insofar as we differentiate other from self.[1]

Interactive preaching by its very nature insists upon a relationally oriented way of valuing, rather than a hierarchical way of valuing. In other words, moving out of the persona requires a shift in value from *what* is being said to *who* is speaking, from the hierarchy of authority to the web of living life contexts. This means that, in order to step down from the pulpit, both physically and in the way we identify with our role as proclaimer, we must come to value finding our place in a web of relationships, rather than valuing the power of being alone at the top.

For instance, consider the authority of the proclaimer from both the perspective of the hierarchy and the web. In the hierarchy, the authority to preach is grounded in the proclaimer's greater experience in the art of preaching, longer study of scripture, broader familiarity in the history of theology, and the high office in the institution. From that perspective, interactive preaching is virtually valueless. But in the model of the web, the authority to preach is grounded in the proclaimer's life context, responsiveness to felt needs, and his or her role in an important network of relationships. From that perspective, interactive preach-

[1]Carol Gilligan, *In a Different Voice: Psychological Theory and Women's Development*. Harvard University Press, 1982, p. 62f.

ing is virtually a necessity. Thus, in preparing to preach interactively, we (both men and women) have to learn to value the authority of our own life contexts.

The persona level by definition shuts out the life context. That is its purpose—to provide the roles in which important social functions (doctoring, policing, governing, ministering) can be performed without the necessity of unraveling the subjective, individual context of each person in the role. *Ex opera operata*, in the old theological doctrine—the function works regardless of the personal circumstances of the one performing the function.

However, at what point does the life context become the crucial question? Precisely where the need for a function stops and the need for a relationship begins. Precisely where it is no longer enough to know that "gospel" is preached, but suddenly where the *context* of the "gospel" being preached must also be known—*who* is preaching and *who* is listening. That is the life context level.

In preparing to preach interactively, we need to be ready to move more fully to the life context level in our preaching. Moving to that level in ourselves means learning to see our sermons not merely as functions but as living personal histories. In fact, what we say in a sermon is grounded in our personal history all the time: grounded in the stresses and pressures of the week, grounded in attitudes and opinions formed precisely out of a specific set of experiences reaching back in time, grounded in our movement through the stages of life. That is why going back through old sermons can be a painful experience: There you see the particular life context because time has created sufficient distance. But it is no less true of next week's sermon.

Engaging the life context means engaging our own history, our own subjectivity. While I want to say a little more practically about how that happens in sermon preparation, for now I just want to notice that a shift of values is required. At the very least, it means preaching more from what we've lived than from what we've read, more from what we have experienced than from what we have been taught, more from what is needed than from what is expected.

And moving beyond the life context level? If preaching out of our life context requires an openness to the subjective context of what we want to say in sermons, then preaching out of the symbolic level requires an openness to the impersonal patterns behind our words and contexts. It requires an eye not only to who is speaking and who is listening in the sermon, but also to the style, pattern, or arrangement in the sermon. If the persona level focuses on content, and the life context level on context, the symbolic level focuses reflection on the correlation, the interrelation of various parts.

For instance, what are the symbolic patterns that shape our preaching? A common image is the wise old man. You will find the wise old man sleeping comfortably in the pages of myth, story, and fairy tale from every age. He is traditionally the one who appears in dangerous times and difficult situations to speak from his wisdom and experience about the right solution. One way of writing a sermon is patterned after the wise old man: A sermon should be wisdom about a difficult situation. Another image, closely related, is the image of the miracle worker: the one with great power who appears at just the right time to transform the situation. A sermon patterned after the miracle worker aims to be the powerful word that transforms. Finally there is the image of the crusader: the one on a mission who defends the cause.

The trouble is, we are not wise old men, or miracle workers, or knights. But these images pattern our sermons in predictable ways, whereas other images would pattern the sermon in new ways: the midwife, the minstrel, the saint, the mother. Preaching out of the symbolic level would require an awareness of the pattern that wants to speak in a given situation, a particular scripture, a liturgical season. It moves our awareness of what is being played out in our preaching to a new level.

What I have been trying to say in a variety of ways is that interactive preaching requires a certain commitment and way of looking at the world. It challenges us to examine not only our values in the enterprise of the sermon, but also our *way* of valuing. In order to preach interactively a minister needs to learn to focus not only on the content of a sermon, but also its context and correlations, its situation and its symbols. It requires an openness to our own subjective experience with the text and the church. Perhaps this is another way of saying that interactive preaching is more pastorally focused, rather than priestly or scholarly. In a manner that is not essential (though certainly still possible) to more traditional preaching, interactive preaching demands a certain orientation to relational experience.

Preparing the Sermon

With that in mind, I want to turn to more practical issues in planning and preparing an interactive sermon. In preparing a traditional sermon, most of us have been taught to concentrate our time on a thorough scholarly investigation of the text—its setting, writer, audience, and history. Perhaps a theme or pattern emerges from which we can choose some illustrations from our favorite books or stories. We then mortar the two together brick by brick, ancient and contemporary.

Play a word association game with the two terms: *construct* and *develop*. The composite picture that emerges for the words associated with "construct" is that of a building site with lumber, bricks, iron, etc., off to the side of a hole in the ground, with a hard-hatted man standing next to a small building with a set of blueprints in his hand....

The composite picture that emerges from words associated with "develop" is something more akin to a several-time double-exposed picture of a rose blossoming. The words used in this case more often than not are words referring to living organic matter (such as "grow," "form," "mature," etc.).

Note that the term "construct" evokes parts-to-whole expressions and "develop" evokes terms associated with living matter processes not separable into distinct parts. This striking difference of evoked association with the two terms is the difference between a static collection of inanimate parts put together to look like a whole on the one hand, and on the other, an organic living whole which is not divisible.[2]

This approach sees the proclaimer more as an artist than as an engineer. It stresses the creative aspect over the ordering aspect. My intuition is that we all approach sermon preparation on the basis of our particular personality types (thinking, feeling, sensation, and intuition). Thus the creative approach relies more on intuition than thinking. However, all of us can learn to let the sermon begin as an expression of an inner idea or image (more introverted), rather than an outer task.

Any description of just how the creative seeds are born goes beyond language. The creative process grows from the depths of the unconscious. Eugene Lowry says:

> There is an incredible gulf between "wandering thoughtfulness" and the "I have it" stage which is difficult to bridge....What I need for a sermon to begin to "happen" is for me to pull my thoughts toward an *intersection point* between the need and the theme....I try to link thoughts from one stack of ideas with the other until a relational gestalt happens.[3]

Something mysterious happens in "wandering thoughtfulness." Many novelists report that their novels grew out of

[2]Eugene Lowry, *The Homiletical Plot: The Sermon As Narrative Art Form*. John Knox Press, 1980, pp. 9-12.
[3]*Ibid.*, pp. 17-19.

some original flash of intuition. The novel represents their attempt to flesh out the full dimensions of that original intuition. The birth of a sermon, like the birth of a novel, needs some flash of intuition.

Lowry's relational gestalt is between two sets of ideas. His most helpful method is aimed at recovering the narrative, the story, the plot aspect of the sermon. For interactive preaching, the relational gestalt we are aiming at is between the text and the listeners that takes place actually during the sermon as the listeners respond.

Thus, we might begin the preparation of an interactive sermon in the same way we begin any sermon, with the text. This should include the full range of scholarship and history available to us. The goal of the historical-critical method is to so distance ourselves from the text, so immerse ourselves in its world, that our own preconceptions fall away. We begin to hear the text in a language and setting foreign from our own. But distance is not interpretation. Interpretation, in the interactive context, is relationship. Understanding the text on its own terms, we need just as importantly to understand the text on our terms. After familiarizing ourselves with the historical context, we have to familiarize ourselves with our own subjective context.

I would point to the notion of the *complex* and the constellation of that complex around the scriptural story in the lives of the listeners as the relational gestalt of interactive preaching. Thus, our task in the preparation of the sermon is to imagine how we might help the interaction unfold along the lines of the complex by the responsive questions we ask the congregation. Remember, it is helpful to think of the complex, as I am using the term here, as a field generated by laying the scriptural story and the life context of the listeners side by side. Life context refers to the stories, images, and feelings that lie behind the way we talk about things (or "see" things, or "feel" about things) and our responses to given situations. Our preparation, then, requires us to familiarize ourselves with the generative field. For instance, in the previous chapter, we saw how the parable of the good Samaritan calls up images of travel, moving down the road, robbers, priests, Levites, etc. The images called up in the personal associations might have to do with travel, helpfulness, response to the poor, enemies, etc. Also, we can include the more collective associations to the situation depicted in the parable such as life passages, traditional religious values, and the shadow or enemy. I suggest that we simply write down as many of our own associations as we have insight to discover. The most important intersection point between the scripture and the life context we are exploring is, at this point, *our own experience* (stories, images, feelings).

I find it helpful to ask myself some key questions: What is my feeling response to the scripture (warm, cold, depression, excitement, etc.)? What are the stories of a couple of experiences I have had that might explain why I respond in this particular way to the text? If I were one of the characters in the story, knowing myself, how would I respond differently than the way they respond? Why? What other images does this story bring to mind? What about this story is important to me? Knowing my own life, how could I predict why I would choose these aspects as important?

From these questions and associations, a good deal of material should unfold. Usually it is possible to begin to group these responses in several different ways. By whatever criteria, we can then begin to choose which of these directions we want to pursue in the sermon. For instance, I might choose to go off in the direction that seems most significant to the congregation at this particular time, or the one that is of greatest interest to me personally at the time.

What we have done by using this method is to begin to get a feel for the field of the complex, or for the life context of this scripture in the life of one person (ourselves). Now knowing the terrain—knowing where we stand, so to speak—we are ready to enter into the "relationship" of this dialogue, and approach the scripture on its own terms once again. The "relationship" consists of the parallels between the scriptural story and our own life context. For instance, in this sermon on the good Samaritan, the parallel may very well be finding ourselves in one of life's passages, perhaps seemingly defeated, and in great need of help from the enemy or shadow aspects of ourselves. Those parallels, that relationship, is the proclamation. Like a complicated chemical interaction, what we have done in this process is to distill the bonding elements of two foreign substances—the text and ourselves—through the heat of our reflection.

Writing an interactive sermon is simply the expansion of that process to include a wider variety of associations. Our own work has given us a familiarity with the field, but we always have to keep in mind that while we may know the context of the scripture before preaching, we do not know the life context of the listener until we ask. So the next step is to frame the interactive questions. The single most important thing to remember about an interactive question, in any of the various types of sermons I will discuss in the next chapter, is the need to build and maintain a relational focus. This relational focus does two important things: It grounds what people say in their own life context (makes it a testimony, an autobiographical statement), and it encourages primary language (stories, feelings, images) rather than didactic, secondary language. The key to shaping the questions is to be sure they ask for life context kinds of data, rather than opinions. That means the questions are phrased in such a way as to evoke a response of a story, feeling, or image. In the sermon of the good Samaritan, we might be tempted to ask questions like: Why do you think Jesus told this story to his listeners? Why do you think the Samaritan helped the man beaten by robbers? Would you have been more like the Samaritan or more like those who passed by on the other side? Upon reflection, none of those questions actually asks for a personal story, feeling, or image. The result of those questions would be a variety of opinions, which can make for argument, but not for dialogue. More truly relational interactive questions might run more in this vein:

Directed question style, feeling oriented, life context level: *What does it feel like to be in the midst of a major transition in your life's journey? Why is it so painful to have to depend on an outsider, or someone very different from yourself, or even an enemy, to get through the transition?*

Shared storytelling style, verbally oriented, life context level: *Can you tell a story about a time in your life when you were caught in the middle of a difficult transition? How did you get through that time? Who came to your aid?*

Symbolic exploration style, visually oriented, symbolic level: *Can you see the beaten, defeated one in you? What does he or she look like? Can you see the stranger, the shadow in you? What does he or she look like?*

In this example, I have stressed the life-stage aspect of the text by focusing on the relationship between the helpless and the helper. This parallels the pericope's grounding in Jesus' attitude toward the enemy. I might just as well have focused on the reversal apparent in the parable and the reaction of Jesus' listeners, the conflict between religious attitudes and daily life that parallels the gospel setting of the story (redaction criticism), or any of a variety of other issues suggested by the text. Also, I phrased each set of questions in one of the three NLP languages. I might just as well have written any of the styles of questions out of a kinesthetic, auditory, or visual reference system, or all three. The crucial consideration is that interactive questions seek to ground the text in the life context and symbolic level of the listeners. We are asking them to make a personal and interpersonal connection with the text.

With our own study and experience in mind, we are ready to write the sermon. I usually write the manuscript out fully, as I would any other sermon. This gives me a chance to see it as a whole, as well as helping find the right places to ask the questions. After it exists in manuscript form, I have found it helpful to outline the sermon on small note cards that I can carry in my hand as I move out of the pulpit. I write the interactive questions out word for word on the note cards because the phrasing needs to be exact.

When actually preaching the sermon, some thought needs to be given to moving through the congregation. A good sound system is important. Ideally, a wireless microphone is best, but a small lavaliere-style microphone works fine, provided the cord is long enough to give free reign. Before preaching the first sermon, some experimentation with the microphone and feedback possibilities needs to be conducted. Other aspects of the worship space need to be considered. In most cases, the placement of the choir during an interactive sermon requires reflection. My own experience found the choir uncomfortable with being so far away from the action. They themselves actually asked to retire from the chancel prior to an interactive sermon. Any obstacles that block the congregation's view need to be avoided. I found it helpful to remind myself not to favor any particular side or place in the sanctuary, being sure to move to the center, down the aisle, to every side.

I have found it important, but not always possible, to move close to the person responding to the sermon. It helps relationally and technically (they can speak into the microphone). I do not find it out of line for the minister sometimes (appropriately) to touch, gesture, or otherwise physically relate to the speaker. When offering a response to a question, sometimes people will raise their hand, and I think it important to call them by their first name. Most people will speak up and take turns quite naturally. Sometimes people misspeak. If someone responds inappropriately, I simply reframe the remark and move on to the next speaker or question.

I would suggest that, probably, interactive preaching should be attempted only after the first year of a new pastorate. It takes time for the relationship between minister and congregation to grow. It also seems wise that a person first really master more traditional preaching styles before attempting interactive preaching. Something like at least two years out of seminary might serve as a guideline. Also, it would obviously be a great advantage to have participated in an interactive sermon before preaching one yourself. My hope would be that all of us might be able to find colleagues who are preaching interactively and to share in a sermon, but also to participate in an informal support group sharing experiences and encouragement. Attending a workshop or a class on interactive preaching would be one of the best preparations.

For all the preparation, there is really no way to predict what will happen in the midst of an interactive sermon. Dialogue, by its very nature, is open. The proclaimer is on the line, and the listeners are as well. No one knows when a question might touch on some of the most formative stories of their life, the most intense feelings, the most powerful images. However, sharing in that depth is the purpose and goal of interactive preaching. The only real preparation is a loving openness to the living complexity of the life context of another human being.

Finally, some thought needs to be given to what happens after the sermon. Given the nature of interactive preaching, I find that people usually cannot avoid making some kind of response to the style itself. More often than not, people respond to the content of a traditional sermon, but with the first use of an interactive sermon, people respond to a style that is probably quite new for them: the preacher out of the pulpit, and asking them to participate. For the most part, the response is positive. Some persons, however, will find that interactive preaching challenges their notion of what a sermon is "supposed" to be. These persons may be other clergy as well. These comments need a full range of pastoral skills in response. We have to be sensitive to the prestige of the pulpit, as well as to a person's natural resistance to painful personal material that an interactive sermon might call up. Exploring the life context of an individual means facing the joyful and the painful, the births and the deaths, the proud and the shameful. The biblical story certainly confronts the real struggles of human life, no less than an interactive sermon that asks people to make a personal connection with "the old, old story." In some cases, the persons who most object to an interactive sermon will be those who have been most touched by the relational experience. In other cases, the objection may simply represent an inability to overcome a deeply rooted attitude toward worship and the sermon. If an interactive sermon violates someone's sense of the sanctity of the pulpit, that person will probably never be able to do more than tolerate interactive sermons in worship.

When a concern is raised, it is particularly important to identify whether the objection comes out of some personal issue that has been stirred by the sermon, or from that person's being generally uncomfortable with the style. If the objection comes out of a personal issue, then it is that issue that needs to be dealt with, rather than interactive preaching. All of our pastoral skills are needed. However, if the objection seems to come more from being uncomfortable with the style, then it is helpful to give the person a chance to identify his or her own understanding of preaching. A common ground can always be found on what is important about preaching, and usually they find it comforting that the minister has not abandoned "preaching" altogether. They need the reassurance that their point of view is valued. That reassurance is usually all they are looking for.

Some consideration must also be given to the feasibility of interactive preaching in regard to the size of the worshiping congregation. I am simply not sure about where to draw the line between "just right" and "too many." In my experience, somewhere between 10 to 20 percent of the congregation will respond to an interactive question (not on the same Sunday) over time. The majority of those remaining will never voluntarily respond. So the value of an interactive sermon does not lie in the number of people who respond in the first place. The value lies in the relational experience created by the few for the many. The value lies in the depth of the stories told from the life context of real people. In congregations of up to one hundred fifty in worship, the size of the congregation is simply not an issue. Where the line lies in larger congregations is difficult to say. I suggest that in settings of five hundred or more, it would be possible to invite a particular group of persons, apart from the congregation, to interact during the sermon. For example, depending on the topic, I could imagine a group of retired clergy, women in ministry, seminarians, lay leaders, homemakers, farmers, etc., interacting with the preacher to the benefit of all.

All in all, interactive preaching is a challenging form of preaching, both for the proclaimer and the listener. As I hope has been made clear from the kind of preparation I have suggested, an interactive sermon may be more work than a traditional sermon. Preaching interactively requires us to research not only the history of the text but our own response to the text as well. While in the course of an interactive sermon we have to be open to whichever course the dialogue may follow, the shaping of the interactive questions gives the sermon as much focus and structure as the three points and a conclusion of a more traditional sermon. Still, the risk of an interactive sermon, as with any sermon, is that something in the gospel story will stir something in the listener's personal story that demands attention and change. From that danger, none of us is safe.

That is the risk of dialogue. That is the risk of being related. When we ask another to tell a story from her life, to step out from behind the mask of the persona, we are asking for a piece of soul to be shared. The risk of true dialogue is that the protective veil that usually hides the vulnerable, vibrant inner life is momentarily lifted, like the cloth over the eucharistic elements. And what is revealed are the sacred artifacts of a lifetime of experience. They glow like fragile candles in the dark recesses of our secret inner life. All of us long with unspoken expectation for someone, someday, to see the meanings we see flickering in our own life, and yet, at the very same time, we fear that if we are truly seen something precious may be lost. In dialogue we reveal something truly precious, but we leave ourselves at the mercy of another who must know the art of handling sacred things. So when we invite dialogue, we also invite responsibility. When we invite ourselves into sacred space, we in the very same moment commit ourselves to be its guardian. What another discloses we are charged to hold forever reverent of the gift. We are then bound to one another.

There can be no dialogue where there is no love to hold it. *Eros* is the only wisdom that can teach us how to hold the pieces of the soul just so, how to love, honor, and cherish the moments of disclosure that commit us to one another. Dialogue brings us to the altar where our stories wed each other. I hold yours, and you hold mine, like trembling hands exchanging rings. That is the relational experience. We cast aside our fear to speak ourselves because the love is greater, the love of living human intimacy that offers greater mystery.

TYPES OF
INTERACTIVE PREACHING

want this chapter to be the practical, "how-to" guts of the book. Not that there is ever a real "how-to" to any form of preaching. With interactive preaching in particular, there must be a receptivity to the unpredictable quality of the relational experience. It requires a certain orientation, theologically and psychologically, on the part of the proclaimer. With this orientation toward a renewed experiential aspect of worship, the how-to will probably come of its own. Without it, no amount of how-to suggestions will help the proclaimer fake a relational experience.

Yet a form-critical analysis is possible, and, I hope, helpful. These forms do not hold up as distinct and pure phenomenological categories. They blend and melt into one another, and have blurry edges. This typology is more practical than philosophical. I will discuss and give examples of four types of interactive sermons: directed questions, shared storytelling, symbolic exploration, and parabling. You may use these types as a springboard to your own ideas and as models for what is possible. In these examples, you will note that many are in the form of a sermon series. I often preach in series because I like the continuity they give from one week to the next, and the way they give people something to expect from me on Sunday morning. They also seem to prevent the pressure of trying to say everything in one sermon.

Directed Questions

The directed question is the most straightforward form of interactive preaching. It can be very much like a traditional sermon, with two major exceptions: It is preached on the same level as the congregation, and there are at least two questions to which the congregation is invited to respond. The importance of physically moving out of the pulpit I have already stressed throughout the book: It closes the relational gap between the pulpit and the pew. It opens up relational space. It is far more visually and kinesthetically stimulating. The importance of the directed question is the new ground the congregation is asked to claim as co-proclaimers.

The sermon begins as any sermon might begin. It exegetes the text. It offers examples and illustrations. It humors, teases, consoles, and inspires. It can even have three points and a stirring conclusion! But choose at least two places in the sermon to ask sharp and narrowly defined questions that are open to response. I generally find that placing the questions in the middle of the sermon is most useful when the proclaimer first introduces the interactive style. People need several minutes of preaching before they are ready to participate. After the congregation is accustomed to the interactive process, beginning a sermon with a directed question coming right out of the scripture is helpful. Ending a sermon with a question is difficult, unless the question truly offers the chance for others to proclaim. (See the example, "In the Upper Room," below.)

The greatest danger of a directed question is that it asks for an opinion. That usually happens because the questions are too global. "What do you think about that?" or "What do you feel about that?" simply asks for a descriptive statement (secondary language). *Therefore let me be certain to define a directed question as a question that asks for a particular set of experiences from the life context level that are recalled, anticipated, or actually recounted in scripture.* In the example, "Living by the Book," the sermon text focuses on John 5:39: "You search the scriptures because you think that in them you have eternal life; and it is they that testify on my behalf." In a Bible study, we might be tempted to ask, "How is it that the scriptures testify on Jesus' behalf?" Such a question calls for interpretive, thinking-oriented language. In an interactive sermon, we ask the question directed toward a particular life context: "How have you tried to live your life by a set of standards and found them inadequate?"

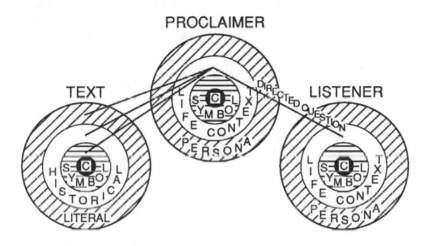

EXAMPLES (from John 5:37–46):

- **Inadequate:** Why do you think Jesus is in such disagreement with the Pharisees? (Too global; asks for an opinion.)

  Better: Do you ever feel that sometimes rules aren't adequate to every situation? (Moving toward feeling language; suggests a life context.)

  Best: How does it feel when you find yourself in a situation where the rules you've been told obviously don't fit anymore? (Specific life context asked for in clear kinesthetic language.)

- **Inadequate:** Do the scriptures really "have eternal life," as Jesus says? (Misses the point; suggests no context.)

  Better: Why does Jesus say there's more to life than the letter of the law? Have you found this to be true in your life? (Tries to move toward a context, but still asks about Jesus, not the listener. In general, avoid asking *why*.)

  Best: Tell me about a time when you put too much emphasis on the letter of the law and regretted it later. (Specific context referred to in auditory language.)

- **Inadequate:** Can you think of some ways in which the scriptures testify on Jesus' behalf, as he says? (No personal connections made.)

  Better: What image of yourself comes to mind when you're struggling with scripture—when you know there's more to it, but just can't see it? (Specific context in visual language.)

  Best: Can you see how you developed the point of view that scripture points to Jesus? Who were some of the people who guided you? (Visual language; reference to a particular situation.)

My experience is that directed questions need to be short, crisply phrased, and delivered twice so that people understand the question. It also takes a little time for the questions to settle in and for the life experiences to come to mind, so don't sweat the silence.

With this type of interactive sermon, I find that my conception of the sermon as a whole, its movement and flow, does not come together until the initial question occurs to me. After that initial ground-breaking question, the next questions become clear and I can begin to antici-pate the direction the interaction might take. It usually takes several hours of sitting patiently with the scripture pondering the connections between the story and my own story. Another helpful approach is to ask, "What is it about this scripture that gets to me, or to which most people respond, *that I can't really put into words?*" (That is really the key.) Then ask a directed question that will give you the answer to that question.

In the examples that follow, I present one complete sermon with two directed questions, just to show how they fit into the flow of the sermon material. Subsequently, I introduce a second sermon and a sermon series only with brief outlines, but I spell out the directed questions.

Example #1. Directed Question Sermon:

A Light Shines in the Darkness

Suggested Scripture: John 1:1–14

It was a clear and lonely night as Edmund Wilson reported for work about 8:00 p.m. In the building where he worked it was cold. Twenty-eight degrees. In fact it was exactly the same temperature in the building as it was outside that cold night, for the temperatures had to be exactly matched to prevent condensation from forming on the lens of the telescope. Edmund Wilson was an astronomer. Throughout the ages, human beings have looked to the stars for wisdom and for mystery. This particular night he was looking into the darkness of space for an object not even visible to the human eye. So faint was its light that it took all night for its light to be gathered and focused by the giant telescope on a tiny photographic plate. As the dawn came, he carefully collected the plate and developed the picture. And what do you think he saw? Not a world, not a star, but a world of stars. Another galaxy. Something so large that it forces us to transcend every concept of time and space known before the twentieth century. Something so large that our own sun is but a single house in the block of the stars visible to us, which is but a single block in the great city of our own galaxy, which is but one city in a million, million other galaxies. That's what Edmund Wilson saw shining through the darkness.

"The light shines in the darkness, and the darkness did not overcome it."

I think that's a key to the scripture and to our faith. Either that light is still shining, maybe weak, but not overcome, or the light has gone out of the world and gone out for humanity. I would propose that there are two sets of human experiences related to the light and darkness: those experiences in which we live as if the night is all of life there is to know, and those experiences of illumination in which life is lived as if the light is truly shining.

Throughout the Gospel of John, people are wrestling with those two experiences. They are looking for a way out

of the darkness. Nicodemus, blinded by his own righteous-
ness. The Samaritan woman at the well thirsting for
something. The hungry multitude looking for the food that
truly satisfies. The man born blind in chapter 9, a key
story. Certainly Mary and Martha and Lazarus. Certainly
even the Pharisees, whom Jesus called blind. Certainly the
disciples—Peter, Andrew, and the rest. They were all
looking for a way out of the darkness.

(Note: moving now into the directed question.) Have
you ever had to live like that? Looking for a way out of the
darkness? Maybe the death of a loved one, a child, an
illness, like cancer or heart disease, or some catastrophe
that just rolls through life like a semi-truck crushing
everything in its wake, maybe like Nicodemus or the
woman at the well? (Directed question, spoken twice:)
What did it feel like for you in the darkest times of your life?

RESPONSES (from an actual sermon)

Man: Back after the flood. (When was that?) Years
ago. Property values were down. Everybody was
moving out. But I didn't want to go. I didn't know
what to do. Couldn't make up my mind. No way to
know what to do.

Woman: When my husband died. That's the hardest thing, you know. When your husband dies. I just
couldn't go on. If it hadn't been for my friends I
think I would have just stopped right then and
there. Most of them are right here in this church.

Second Woman: This is hard. I don't know how to
say this. I don't think people know. I mean, when I
was 19, well, it was black, really black. I was on
drugs (pause). I was really messed up (stops). (I
give her time, and then say I'll come back to her).

(Does anyone else want to add anything?)

Man: Yes, well, sure, there are hard times in life.
The darkest time? Well I guess that would be...well,

I was gonna say right now, but you know, it's been worse. I want to say it must have been when I was in the war. That was pretty bad. I'd never been so scared. Never knew if I was gonna live or die. So I guess I'm glad to be alive today.

"The light shines in the darkness, and the darkness did not overcome it."

In the gospel they all come asking for a way out of the darkness: Nicodemus, the Samaritan woman, the blind man, and the rest. And the point is that Jesus offers a light. He knows their lives better than they know them themselves and in every conversation he points the way out. "You must be born from above," he said to Nicodemus (John 3:7). "The water that I will give will become in them a spring of water gushing up to eternal life," he said to the Samaritan woman (John 4:14). "I am the light of the world," he said to the blind man (John 9:5).

John 12:46: "I have come as light into the world, so that everyone who believes in me should not remain in the darkness."

There is a light in you that will never go out. That we have as a promise from the Light of the World. In you, in me, in the soul of the most unenlightened person who ever walked the earth, there is a light that will never go out. Children have it. Saints have it. You and I have it, although we often get so far away from it that it is visible to us only through a powerful telescope. But we have it. Deep inside. And I don't mean consciously, something you can find in yourself if you just try hard. Something deep inside our deepest selves. Something perhaps we only catch a glimpse of two or three times in a lifetime, or in our dreams. Something we see only in those moments when our spiritual eyes learn to gaze upon our naked souls.

(Note: moving into the directed question.) In those moments of darkness you've just been talking and thinking about, where was the light? (Directed question:) *What did you touch within yourself when you reached the bottom and found you could feel your way in the darkness?*

RESPONSES

Man: I was laid off once. Hard times. Didn't know if we'd make it through, you know, if we'd lose the house or whatever. I was real depressed. But one morning, I don't know what it was, I just woke up and I knew everything was gonna be all right. Don't know why it happened. Don't know if it was God or anything like that. I think it was. I mean I was just out of gas one day, and the next day I woke up and I knew it was gonna be all right. And it was, you know. Just worked out.

Woman: You just find it within yourself. You just reach down and find something there. (Do you remember what it felt like?) Yes. Like a miracle. That's what I call it. I had pins in both my knees and they said I'd never walk. But I did. I knew I could do it. And it was only with the help of God.

Second Woman (from before): (Are you ready?) It's OK. I just want to say it all changed. I just realized there was more to me than that. I just started to care about myself as a person. (You found something within yourself?) I found my life. I wanted to live. And I also found God. I mean, I went to church before. But for the first time I found God. Do you know what I mean? Finding God was discovering there's more to life than just yourself.

Woman: I think you find it in your friends. I think this church is like that. People care about you and help you and that's what makes it better. You don't have to be alone. Your friends care about you. (What did you find in yourself?) Love maybe. If you find how to love, it's all right.

Thank you. Thank you all. I just want you to remember what it was like when the night was dark and what it was that got you through it. I just want you to remember that if you've found something within yourself once, you will find it again. A light within us. I believe that for far too long, Western Christianity has looked far and wide for the transcendent God. The God above planets and stars and galaxies. The God who is outside of all creation. But the saints have known, and those who have sought the inner life of the Spirit have known, that the God we seek is closer than we have ever imagined. The God within. The immanent God. The God who became flesh and dwelt among us, full of grace and truth.

Example #2. Directed Question Sermon:

In the Upper Room
Suggested Scripture: Luke 14:12–26

I. Guided meditation on the text

I want to begin this evening with a meditation. So let me ask you all to close your eyes. You can bow your head if you like. I want you to alter your breathing, breathing in slowly, exhaling slowly. Deeply in, slowly out. Clear your mind so that you see nothing but a gray screen. Now slowly I want you to let the image of that upper room form. Let the room itself appear first. Try and see the floor—its color, its material. Now see where it meets the wall and the color of the wall. Follow the wall around until you can see the entire room. Now the furniture. What do you see? Let that be firmly in place. Hold it in your imagination.

Slowly I want you to see who is in the room. Start first with the color of the clothes. Now I want you to see whether they are sitting or standing. How tall they are. What does it smell like in that room? What sounds do you hear? I particularly want you to get a feel for the emotional atmosphere in the room. What's the situation, as if you were there too? Finally, I want you to see Jesus himself. Let whatever appears come. See his clothes. See his face. (Long pause.) Now, very slowly, I want you to come back to this time and place. (Pause.)

What happened in your meditation?

RESPONSES

Man: It was different than I expected. You know, different than the painting. I could really see them. And they didn't have beards!

Woman: Yes, it was different. In mine there was this tree in the middle. I don't know why it was there. And the biggest part was the roots. (That's remarkable). Yes. The tree seemed very important.

Woman: Well, I couldn't really get a picture to come. But I could see the communion on the table, the bread and the wine. That was very clear. Very moving.

(No one has said anything about Jesus.)

Woman: I think it's hard, you know, hard to see the Savior. I was kind of scared. I didn't want to do that part. (Did you see him?) Yes. He was, well, nice. But troubled. Like at a funeral. That's just what it reminded me of. Like what people look like when they go to the funeral home.

II. Exposition
(Here, I offer an account of a few of the details of the Jewish rite of passover, provide a brief exegesis of the text, and mention finally the events that followed immediately after the Last Supper.)

III. Directed questions
Now I want you to put yourself back in the picture you made during the meditation. Remember the emotional atmosphere in the room. Remember what is yet to come. Now, knowing the situation in that room on that night, I want to ask you an important question. *What would you say to Jesus? What would you want him to hear from you?*

RESPONSES

Woman: I want you not to suffer. I want you not to hurt. It's not right. You're too good to suffer.

Man: Have courage, have hope. We are with you. Don't give up. You have a mission and if you can just get through this, you will save the world.

Woman: I thank you, I love you. I rejoice in what you are doing for me. Thank you for giving yourself up for me. I will follow you always.

(Other responses.)

Thank you. Those are important statements. Now, still in that upper room, I want you to imagine that in this private conversation with him, he has heard you. Tell me now, *how do you think Jesus would respond to you? What would he say?*

RESPONSES

Woman: He would say, "You must not fear to suffer. You must bear your pain as I bear mine. I go to my Father and I am not afraid. Be not afraid."

Man: I know what he would say. He's not like me. He would say "I must walk my road alone, as you must walk yours. I carry the cross and you carry a cross too. God will help you."

Woman: He tells me, "You do not know what I am doing." And he's right. We can't know what he's doing. We can't ever really understand what it must have been like for him. I think he would say "You do not know the cost."

(Other responses.)

IV. Conclusion

Thank you. I am surprised. I am surprised at the way it feels like he has really spoken this evening. From what you've said, it's clear that Jesus' wisdom is a deeper wisdom than our own. In response to us, his perspective is always so different from our own perspectives. His way of seeing things is so different from our way. I am always amazed that Jesus consistently speaks to us from his commitment to the kingdom of God. To a deeper way of life. I invite you to think on what has been said here this evening. I invite you to continue this conversation with Jesus in the privacy of your own inner thoughts. I invite you to remember this experience of the upper room as we come around this holy table, as we hear the words he spoke, taste of the bread and cup he offered, seek the presence that he is....

(Movement to the communion service.)

Example #3. Directed Question Sermon Series:
The Passion for Life

First Sermon:

The Passion for Life: Living by the Book

Suggested Scripture: Exodus 32:1–4, 15–16; 34:4–7;
Ephesians 2:8–12; John 5:37–46

I. Introduction
  A. Explanation of the interactive sermon process.
  B. Introduction to the series. (The next three weeks we'll be looking at three different ways of living life religiously, living by the book, living by the heart, living by joy, etc.)

II. Rules
  A. Story about childhood rules and the things we teach our children.
  B. The children of Israel had many rules: Ten Commandments, four entire books of rules, more than three thousand ordinances.
  C. Did they live happily ever after? See Exodus 32:7–8. They made the golden calf.
  D. All of us have also been given many rules to live by: our culture, masculinity and femininity, our parents.
  E. Directed question: *What were some of the rules your parents told you to live by?*

III. Living by the book
  A. The promise is: Living by the book will give you life.
  B. Isn't the Bible a book to live by?
  C. John 5:39—"You search the scriptures because you think that in them you have eternal life; and it is they that testify on my behalf."
  D. What can those words mean?
  E. How can we live without a book of rules? Can we live without them?

F. Jesus and the Pharisees. Paul and the Law. Martin Luther and the church, all fighting against hiding in the letter of the law.

G. Key: Religious life is not in the letter of the law, but in the Spirit. Eternal life is not in the scripture but in the presence of Christ. Religious life is not a matter of "morality," but a matter of relationships.

IV. Road maps

A. By the age of twenty or so, each of us has formed a road map in our heads of the way life is supposed to be.

B. That road map is formed by our culture, our family, our experience.

C. That road map tells us whom to trust, what to risk, what will make us happy, whom to love.

D. The problem is, nine times out of ten, that road map is inaccurate.

E. Story of a woman with an inaccurate life map.

F. Directed question: *How have you tried to live your life by a set of standards and found them inadequate?*

V. Conclusion

A. Story of Gobo Fraggle and Uncle Mat's Book for Exploring.

B. At judgment day, I stand before God and say, "I have lived by the book all of my life." God says, "But where is the book you were to have written with your own life?"

Example #4. Directed Question Sermon Series:
The Passion for Life

Second Sermon:
The Passion for Life: Living by the Heart

Suggested Scripture: Jeremiah 31:31–34;
Ephesians 3:14–19;
John 1: 15-17, 25–27

I. Directed question
  A. This passage in John talks about the Holy Spirit....
  B. Directed Question: *How do you know when you feel the presence of the Holy Spirit?*

II. The Holy Spirit in the Gospel of John

III. Transcendent or immanent experience of the divine?
  A. John 14:17: "You know him, because he abides with you, and he will be in you."
  B. Shocking statement, "will be in you."
  C. Biblical scholarship has tended to be extraverted and emphasize a transcendent view of God.
  D. But there is equal emphasis in the Bible on an immanent view of God (Luke 17:20–21, Ephesians 3:16, Romans 8:11).
  E. Directed question: *Do you feel God's presence more as an outer God or an inner God?*

IV. The term *heart*
  A. Popular biblical term, used 978 times in scripture by my count.
  B. Heart is a metaphor of the deepest seat of the life of the psyche: the seat of emotions but also of intellect and will (volition).
  C. Heart is a metaphor for that place within us that is a point of contact with God.
  D. Perhaps the best translation for heart would be "personality." Eph. 3:17: "...that Christ may dwell

in your *personality* through faith."

E. Better yet, translate as "deepest inner self," as in Jeremiah 31:33: "I will put my law within them, and I will write it on their *deepest inner selves.*"

F. Jeremiah's new covenant.

V. Living by the heart

A. Living by the heart does not mean living with your emotions on your sleeve.

B. Living by the heart means guiding your life by your commitment to that deepest inner self.

C. For example, decision making: Living by the heart would mean doing what is most meaningful and purposeful rather than what is "best" and acceptable.

D. Second example, the experience of illness: Living by the heart would mean asking, "What is wrong in my life now that needs changing? What is my deepest self saying through my illness?" rather than trying to be cured so that you may go on living as before.

E. Third example, the mission of the church: Living by the heart would mean the invitation for experience of the sacred, rather than the focus on teaching about experience of the sacred.

F. Directed question: *What did it feel like in those moments in your life when you were living by the heart?*

VI. Conclusion

A. Living by the heart is neither easy nor safe.

B. Looking within ourselves, we find light and darkness, good and evil.

C. But pilgrims have taken up the quests throughout history: the holy grail, the pearl of greatest value, the treasure hidden in a field.

Example #5. Directed Question Sermon Series:
The Passion for Life

Third Sermon:
The Passion for Life: Living By Joy

Suggested Scripture: Jeremiah 31:10–14;
Ephesians 2:17–22;
John 15:1-5, 8–11

I. Introduction
   A. Brief review of the interactive sermon experience during the series.
   B. Living by joy is a way of life that few people ever achieve and an experience that is difficult to communicate.
   C. If living by the book is the wager that we can find life by living according to someone else's rules, and if living by the heart is the quest for what lies hidden within us, then living by joy is the joy of finding what is living within us.
   D. Joy is the bedrock, the payoff, abundant life as it is actually experienced.

II. Persons who lived by joy
   A. Jeremiah lived by the heart, but in the end learned to live by joy.
   B. After the fall of Jerusalem, his darkest moment, he experienced joy: Jeremiah 31:12–14.
   C. Story of a very inhibited woman in therapy who learned to dance. "Then shall the young women rejoice in the dance, and the young men and the old shall be merry" (Jeremiah 31:13).
   D. Directed question: *Can you think of an experience in which you saw in that moment that you were doing something you were meant to do, created to do?*

III. Living by joy means being connected
   A. Ephesians offers another example of living by joy.

B. Surprising paradox: By reaching deep inside of ourselves, we discover just how much we are connected to other people.

C. Ephesians 2:19: "So then you are no longer strangers and aliens, but you are citizens with the saints and also members of the household of God."

D. Joy comes from the experience of deep immersion in the inner self, which surprisingly reveals that we are ultimately not alone.

E. Directed question: *Can you see yourself in a moment, perhaps painful and personal, in which you discovered that you were not as alone as you thought you were?*

IV. Jesus lived by joy

A. In his farewell speech, Jesus found joy in living his life as he knew God intended him to live.

B. He also found joy in discovering he was not alone, but ultimately connected to those he called "friends" (John 15:13).

C. But living by joy ultimately means "abiding" (John 15:5).

D. John 15:11: "I have said these things to you so that my joy may be in you, and that your joy may be complete."

E. Living by joy means finding that your life is not your own but that the energy, the power, the zest for living, come from a deeper source.

F. Abiding is as easy (and as difficult) as opening up our inner veins so that the sap can flow.

V. Conclusion: surprised by joy

C. S. Lewis writes in his book *Surprised by Joy*:

In introspection we try to look "inside ourselves" and see what is going on. But nearly everything that was going on a moment before is stopped by the very act of our turning to look at it. Unfortunately this does not mean that introspection finds nothing. On the contrary, it finds precisely what is left behind by the suspension of all our normal activities; and what is left behind is mainly mental images and physical sensations...like the swell at sea, working after the wind has dropped.

This discovery flashed a new light back on my whole life. I saw that all my waitings and watchings for Joy, all my vain hopes to find some mental content on which I could, so to speak, lay my finger and say, "This is it," had been a futile attempt....I knew now that they were merely the mental track left by the passage of Joy—not the wave but the wave's imprint on the sand....

And that is why we experience Joy: we yearn, rightly, for that unity which we can never reach except by ceasing to be the separate phenomenal beings called "we." Joy was not a deception. Its visitations were rather the moments of clearest consciousness we had, when we became aware of our fragmentary...nature and ached for that impossible reunion.[1]

[1]C.S. Lewis, *Surprised by Joy: The Shape of My Early Life*. Harcourt, Brace, and Jovanovich, 1955, pp. 218-222.

Shared Storytelling

Shared storytelling is probably the most interactive form of preaching. By shared storytelling, I mean a sermon in which the proclaimer asks the congregation to share stories around a particular life context suggested by the scripture. The sermon is the stories. Such contexts might include: birth, religious experience, dreams, renewal, building programs, hospital experiences, weddings—and the list goes on as far as one's imagination. The proclaimer introduces the context, usually shares a story of his or her own, and opens the floor to others. After each story, he or she might comment briefly to the storyteller, affirming the gift of the story. At the end of the appointed time, the proclaimer might bring together a few of the leitmotifs and close with prayer.

There may be no exegesis. There may be no formal structure, although prior to the stories there might be an introduction and, following them, a conclusion. Is it still a sermon? Yes! In so far as a sermon is the proclamation of the "good story," the story of God's presence in our lives, shared storytelling is sermonic. A story told in the context of worship is a proclamation. The stories told are revelations-in-relationship. They are testimonies in the most positive sense of the word. They are not "sermons" only if sermons must be confined to secondary language about experience. But if sermons are a language event, then in the very telling of the stories, good news (authentic human experience) is proclaimed.

The difference between a directed question sermon and a shared storytelling sermon lies in the focus. Both ask questions aimed at the life context level in the listener. But the directed questions constellate a life context in the midst of which *the proclaimer* speaks the word, makes the proclamation. In shared storytelling, to my mind, the life context of *storyteller* is the proclamation. The storyteller speaks the word.

My experience has been that shared storytelling is a celebrative event. Even when the stories are stories of struggle and pain, in the telling the experience becomes a celebration of having lived to tell the story. Because of their special "event" quality, shared storytelling sermons are probably best used sparingly and on special occasions, although the event itself will make an otherwise ordinary Sunday a special occasion. People will remember and find meaning in the stories told in worship far longer than the three points of last week's sermon.

Example #6. Shared Storytelling Sermon:

Life-Affirming Stories About Death

Suggested Scripture: Psalm 121;
Romans 5:1–5; John 14

Suggested Occasion: Memorial Day
or All Saints Day

I. Introduction

We are sharing in a special occasion this morning, remembering those who were friends and partners and family to us. Remembering those who have already experienced the mystery of death. Throughout the centuries we have always remembered our dead, believing that they share with us in worship in the great "communion of the saints." Believing that our deeper life in the mystery of Christ continues, one great church on earth and in heaven, the saints below and the saints above.

I'm aware that in my own life, death has been a mystery. There are stories about those deaths and the way people I love have died. Those experiences have been an inspiration, mysterious, scary, but deeply meaningful to me. I want to share a couple of those stories with you. My guess is that you also have meaningful stories you might want to share.

What's the point of these stories? The stories we tell about an experience to a large part determine how we will understand and live out that experience. The life-affirming stories that you have experienced are gifts. They are stories your brother and sister Christians need to hear. All of these stories together form a rich heritage and treasure all of us can draw upon in times of need. Those stories can become like a "great cloud of witnesses" that strengthen all of us to run the race with perseverance. I invite you to spend a few minutes right now letting those experiences, sights, sounds, and feelings, return to your mind.

II. The proclaimer's stories

(At this point the proclaimer may share one or two stories from his or her own life which should set the tone for the material to follow. I might tell a story of playing the organ at the first funeral I ever attended, or about the bouquet of roses that the wind blew off the coffin just as we were reciting the Lord's Prayer saying "lead us not into temptation but deliver us from evil," or a dream my mother had about her own mother returning to talk with her about death.)

III. Stories told from the congregation

(Interactive question:) *What stories do you remember about strange things that felt meaningful at the time of a death?* (The proclaimer should invite stories from the congregation. Many people will quite naturally stand, even turn around, to tell their story from the pew. If they don't stand or speak up, encourage them to do so. If a microphone can reach far enough, the proclaimer should share the microphone with them. Note: Some people will tell deeply moving stories at this point and it seems appropriate to me that the proclaimer comfort, touch, or otherwise respond, silently, to the feelings being expressed. This should be done in a way that encourages folks to continue the story through to the end, for the healing is in the movement of the story from beginning to end. Occasionally someone begins a story but is simply unable to continue, and the proclaimer should affirm the need to stop at that point and move to another story. Be sure to check out the experience with the person after the service and work through any unresolved feelings. After each story, the proclaimer should make a few remarks, briefly summarizing the point of the story, or accurately naming the feeling. For instance, "I can see from that story that this was a difficult experience for you, but that you grew as a person in the experience." My experience has been that if the sermon is to be kept to twenty minutes and the stories are full-fledged stories, there is time only for six or seven stories. But every person in the congregation will have a story come to mind.)

IV. Conclusion

(Particularly with this sermon, which opens up a deep level of feeling, it is important to conclude with some sort of liturgical movement that functions to contain and appropriately close off the experience. My suggestion is that some sort of liturgy for the dead be read at this point, which should include ample congregational response. I have typically read the names of members of the congregation who have died in the last year, making brief comments about each, just before the liturgy. It is very meaningful if the congregation can participate in communion immediately following the sermon. In this setting the communion becomes, quite appropriately, a requiem.)

Example #7. Shared Storytelling Sermon:

Glimpses

Suggested Scripture: Luke 18:18–30
or Matthew 28:16–20

Suggested Occasion: Stewardship emphasis
or evangelism emphasis

I. Introduction

As we are thinking about our stewardship of all that God has given us during this season, I wonder if you've ever stopped to think just how wonderful and powerful a gift the people sitting in the pews with you are in your life? The love, caring, support, these people have given you through the years? How much could we pay for such a gift? How would we find it in the yellow pages, or arrange a loan to pay for it? How would we ever find and obtain what we receive from one another? Have you ever thought about that?

I want to concentrate this morning on what it is that binds us together in the first place. What it is that we are giving for. In a very real sense, I don't know. I mean, I know from how we have talked from time to time about just what this congregation means to you, and I'm sure that I know stories about your brothers and sisters in the pews that most of you don't know. But in actuality, we just won't know what the appeal of this place is unless we name it with each other.

We often take it for granted: what it is that binds us together. I know that we don't often talk about it, because we assume that glue is self-evident.

What I want to do this morning is to make those basic assumptions and feelings about our life together clear. Not any single one of us has the whole thing. We have our piece of it. We have our "glimpse" of what it is that's underneath us, but we don't have the whole puzzle.

So what I want to do this morning is to have you share the various "glimpses" of our life together in the hope that as we hear from one person after another, all of us might begin to get a larger picture of the meaning this congregation has for the people who live its life.

II. Stories from the congregation

(In this sermon we ask a question or a couple of questions. These might be helpful:) *If you were to use one word that best describes your experience in this congregation, what would it be?* (This should be the first question, going around the room for maybe ten or fifteen one-word responses). *Can you think of a time when you felt most cared for by this congregation? What is one of your most important memories of something that touched you personally? If you were trying to tell someone who had never been to this church what felt right about it to you, what story would you give as the best illustration?*

Please note that these questions ask specifically for *experiences*, rather than for reasons or explanations. It is important in shared storytelling to make sure the questions are phrased in such a way that primary language emerges, rather than secondary, deductive language. Also note that the questions should be personally directed, something that actually happened in the life of the person telling the story, rather than "hearsay" or second-hand stories.

III. Conclusion

(Again, there is a need for the right kind of liturgical movement to signal that the storytelling experience and the feelings expressed are ready to be closed off. An affirmation of faith, or a reading of a congregational statement of purpose can fulfill this role.)

Symbolic Exploration

With a symbolic exploration style of interactive sermon, we move to another level. The questions in this style set out intentionally to aim at the symbolic level of the listener. One might say that while the directed question and shared storytelling style make the amplification of the text from the life context of the listener, the symbolic exploration calls for an amplification of the text from the inner figures, connecting the biblical symbols and characters through the parallel personifications in each of us. For instance, rather than a sermon *about* the prodigal son, the symbolic exploration sermon asks, "Who is the prodigal in you?" Symbolic exploration, then, has to do with the real parallels between our inner characters and attitudes with those symbolized and portrayed in scripture.

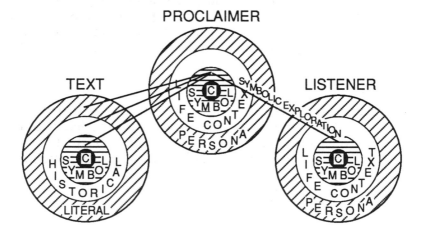

TEXT: Parable of the Prodigal Son

- **Directed question:** *Can you remember what it felt like to want to leave home?*

  Shared storytelling question: *Tell us a story about leaving home for the first time.*

Symbolic exploration question: *Who is the prodigal in you? What does he (she) want?*

- **Directed question:** *Who do you see in your own life as a parent waiting for you to return?*

Shared storytelling question: *Parents, can you tell a story about a time when you were very worried about what was going on with one of your children?*

Symbolic exploration question: *In what situations are you in your parental attitude? What are your concerns? What are your priorities when you're like that?*

- **Directed question:** *What are your thoughts when you are left out like the elder brother? What words come to mind?*

Shared storytelling question: *Can you think of a time when you were just too proud to join in someone else's celebration? What happened?*

Symbolic exploration question: *Imagine you are the one who stayed home. What are your rights, what is your claim? In what situations does your elder brother come out in you?*

Symbolic exploration sermons offer a method to make the interpretive goal of "participation"—the connection to the text that makes "appropriation" possible—actually happen in worship. Participation in this sense means that we surrender our box seats as simply readers over against the text, and move down to the stage as characters included in the drama. Walter Wink introduced the method back in the 1970s out of his association with the Guild for Psychological Studies in San Francisco.[2] Wink's method is designed for a group context, but I have found it parallels my own ideas for preaching.

---

[2]Walter Wink, *The Bible in Human Transformation: Toward a New Paradigm for Biblical Study.* Fortress Press, 1973.

Wink offers a helpful description of the method, using a study of the healing of the paralytic (Matthew 9:1–8; Mark 2:1–12; Luke 5:17–26). He works with the group as a leader, using three lines of questioning. In the first round, he deals with the historical-critical issues in the text: comparing the different synoptic versions of the paralytic story, a form-critical issue (both a conflict and a healing story), etc. This is the kind of approach we might be familiar with. But the next exploration we might find a little different. In the second round of questions, Wink focuses on working with the story *as a story,* i.e. the questions aim at getting us to identify with the human elements in the story: What about the friends carrying the paralytic? What might they be feeling as they approach? What do they do with their initial disappointment? What is the attitude of the paralytic toward his own healing? What does he really want? What is Jesus' attitude as he confronts the sick man? What is the scribe's attitude? How are they different? These questions bring us closer to a human element in the story. Biblical criticism tells us that trying to enter the story ourselves is unhistorical, since we have no way of knowing those personal sorts of motivations. What we say is simply our own *imagination* working on the text. I would say that such an engagement of imagination is critical for any kind of interpretation that is going to be helpful to us in the long run anyway: the appropriation of the story through our own life context. This second line of questioning brings us imaginatively into the story ourselves. That is the life context level.

But the third line of questioning goes another step. We imagine not only that we are in the story, but, in order to take it to a symbolic level, we try to imagine all of the characters in the story as different aspects of our own personality. Wink offers this example:

Q.—Who is the "paralytic" in you? That is to say, with what aspect of yourself does this character resonate, if any? (long pause)

A.—It is the way I've been over-academized. The way I reduce everything to an intellectual exercise.

—It's the suppressed power I have as a woman, which is only allowed expression as bitchiness. Women weren't—aren't—supposed to have strength.

—It's the loss of my whole feeling side, my incapacity as a man to know how I feel about things that happen....

Q.—Now, who is the "scribe" in you?

A.—It's the part of me that is always judging me, making me feel unworthy.

—My "scribe" is my intellectualism. My theologian. My skeptic.

—The "scribe" in me is saying it doesn't like what you're doing in this discussion.

—It's the part of me that can think well of myself only by repressing all knowledge of the injured, imperfect, or evil parts of me. So it hates me for having a paralytic, and does everything in its power to keep it down.

Q.—But why doesn't the "scribe" want the "paralytic" healed—both in you and in the story?

A.—Because he can't admit that this too is a part of him. He wants too badly to think well of himself....

Q.—So what is the relationship between the "scribe" and the "paralytic"?

A.—Well, the paralytic is as bad off as the scribe, since he's internalized the scribe's judgment of him as being accurate....

(The period ends. Each participant is given a bag of clay and asked to model their "paralytic" or their "scribe" in the light of the day's discussion and bring it to the next seminar.)[3]

---

[3]*Ibid.*, pp. 56-60.

Several observations need to be made in translating this method into a symbolic exploration sermon. Primarily, in a sermon we lack the time to explore the number of symbolic questions that Wink suggests, and that arise naturally from any text. My suggestion is that we choose five critical questions, or that we spread the sermon out into two or three sermons in a series (one on the paralytic, one on the scribe, one on the healer). Also, the use of the assignment to model the characters in clay is an essential feature of Wink's method. We do not truly appropriate inner figures unless we relate them to the conscious part of ourselves through clay, art, poetry—any vital, connecting link that makes the relationship between the conscious and unconscious part of ourselves concrete. Although it would obviously be difficult to require such a working through in the context of worship, I see no reason that an invitation cannot be made for the congregation to continue the "work" through the week.

My method makes more use of guided meditation. It is essential for a symbolic exploration sermon that the scripture and the sermon be directly related. So I suggest that the scripture reading and the sermon be one joint moment in worship. Move down from the pulpit for the reading of the scripture. Introduce the context of the pericope in the story. Invite all to close their eyes and alter their breathing. Spend the proper amount of time on this centering as one would do with any spiritual discipline. Then ask the congregation to enter imaginatively into the moment of the pericope. Explain that you want them to pay attention to the details of the moment, being sure that you point out visual, auditory, and feeling details to be kept in mind: What are they wearing, are they seated or standing, how tall are they, what do they sound like, what sounds are heard, what is the emotional climate of the situation, what does it feel like to be there, etc.? The more details that can be imagined, the more concrete the meditation becomes. Then read the scripture, preferably in the present tense. In the story of the paralytic (Mark 2:1–12):

He has returned to Capernaum after some days, and it is reported he is at home. So many have gathered around that there is no longer room for them, not even in front of the door; and he is speaking the word to them. Now some people come, bringing to him a paralyzed man, carried by four of them. And when they cannot bring him to Jesus because of the crowd, they remove the roof above him....

Following the scripture reading, invite the congregation to come back slowly to the time and place of worship. I often spend just a few minutes asking folks to share what they saw, heard, and felt during the meditation, asking about which details in particular surprised them.

The next movement is into the body of the sermon. This is the place for any form-critical, redactional, or literary analysis you want to make. In my sermon on the paralytic I might describe the form of a miracle story and the role of the scribes in Jesus' day.

With all of that in place, we are ready to move into the symbolic exploration. Some kind of transitional statement is required. It is important that the transition stay as close as possible to the scripture, while at the same time suggesting the symbolic parallel. I might say something like this:

I have to admit I'm more like the scribe than I often care to realize. I mean, sometimes I cling tightly to my own sense of right and wrong, proper and improper, inbounds and out of bounds. It's hard for me to be confronted with someone who values what I value but goes about it in a completely different way. Do you see what I mean?

The first symbolic exploration question follows immediately: *Who is the scribe in you?* At this stage, the stories begin, and once the process is happening there is little need to intervene, but simply to focus the next symbolic exploration question and keep track of the time. My series of questions would be a little different than Wink's. I focus more strongly on the scribe. The second question might be:

Who is the paralytic in you (how are you sometimes paralyzed)? Then: *How does your scribe need the paralytic? How does Jesus aim at healing the scribe? Why or how does your scribe block the healing Jesus is trying to give?*

I find that the material for the short concluding statement comes right out of wrestling with the text and wrestling with ourselves, so I generally do not prepare a conclusion to a symbolic exploration sermon. In this example, it might run something like this:

> I think we've seen this morning just how strong the
> scribe still is. I really like the way you've said that
> it is so hard to make room for the irrational when
> we're all taught to be so rational and logical (and
> hard-headed!). But of course we are confronted
> with the irrational all the time: in the hospital, at
> deaths, the unexpected miracles and disasters of
> daily life—all of those things that challenge our
> sense of what's proper and ought to be. But I think
> we found that the healing element had to do with
> Jesus' offer to the scribe to see the humanity of the
> person right before his eyes, to hear the need of the
> paralytic and feel his suffering. But to do that, the
> scribe would have to confront his own paralysis,
> wouldn't he? He freezes up when confronted with
> the paralytic. So do we. Our sense of what ought to
> be freezes us sometimes when we come up against
> what really is. Maybe that's the key, like one of you
> said. Learning to face up to what really is, painful
> as it might be, is the first step to our own healing.

I hope that this extended example provides a sense of how a symbolic exploration sermon flows. And it must flow. The opening meditation is crucial in creating the reflective tone necessary for the questions. The grounding of the sermon in a real inner figure, as a result of the first question, opens up space for what happens in the questions that follow. I find that this style of sermon requires a lot of preparation. The sequence of questions must be chosen with great care. The phrasing of the questions needs to be specific (not global). It is important that the questions emerge from the text, not arbitrarily from the proclaimer. (And the questions are there to be found in the text!) For me, a symbolic exploration sermon does not quite come together until I have understood the challenge of the pericope in my own life context.

Example #8. Symbolic Exploration Sermon:

Three Women's Experiences of Jesus

Suggested Scripture: John 4:7–15;
John 8:3–11; Luke 7:34–50

I. Introduction

I think you will find this is an unusual set of scriptures to put together. They are not usually set side by side. But, unless I miss my guess, I think we can learn a thing or two about women and about Jesus by looking at all three together.

It's kind of strange, actually. The very first place I saw these three women put together is in the great epic poem of the German language, Goethe's "Faust." These three women—the woman at the well, the woman caught in adultery, and the woman who wept at Jesus feet—are said to be, by Goethe, among the first three people Faust meets when he gets to heaven. Think of it. Instead of being met by Saint Pete, Goethe imagines that we might be met by three sinning women, each forgiven by Jesus himself.

II. Scripture reading

(For this sermon I ask the congregation to read the scriptures, printed in the bulletin, rather than a guided meditation. I ask them to read it in this manner: With the story of the woman at the well, I ask the women in the congregation to read the words spoken by the woman, the men to read the words spoken by Jesus, and I read the narration. With the story of the woman caught in adultery, the same arrangement is followed, women reading the one line of the woman, men reading Jesus, I read the narration. But with the reading of the woman at Jesus' feet, I switch the roles—and this is important—with the men reading the part of the Pharisees, the women reading the words of Jesus, while I read the narration.)

III. Exposition

A. Historical notes: John 8:3–11 is not part of most manuscripts and moves around; historically, these three women are sometimes thought of as being the same person, Mary Magdalene.

B. Notice that all three women are historically thought to have committed sins of a sexual nature (whether explicit in scripture or not).

C. Notice that in each case there is a group of men who stand in judgment.

D. Notice that in each case Jesus engages in a relationship with these women that he really shouldn't be in and for which he is condemned.

E. Historical notes on the role of women in society in Jesus' times.

IV. Symbolic exploration

A. *In what situations do you tend to act like the Pharisees and scribes catching a sinner?*

B. *What words would you use to describe the pharisaical attitude in yourself?*

C. *How is the way Jesus listens and responds to these women different from the other men?*

D. *What is it in you that makes your attitude toward "sinners" so different from Jesus'?*

E. *How does the sinner in you feel when confronted with the Pharisees?*

F. *How does the sinner in you feel about Jesus?*

V. Conclusion
(Weave together the elements of the responses, being sure to note the connection between the Pharisees and our

attitude toward sinners, between the women and our attitude toward ourselves as sinners, and the resolution of the conflict between the "righteous" and sinners that Jesus offers.)

Example #9. Symbolic Exploration Sermon Series on the Birth Narratives

First Sermon:
Lessons on Being Pregnant

Suggested Scripture: Luke 1:26–38

I. Guided meditation on Luke 1:26–38

II. Exposition
(Some reflections: Note the emphasis on Mary and feminine figures in Luke 1; the Gospel of Luke tells us more about Mary than any other gospel; the so-called "annunciation pattern" of (1) the appearance (of angel or God to Abraham, Moses, Zechariah, Joseph, and Mary), (2) a reaction of fear (in all the above stories), (3) an announcement, (4) an objection, and (5) the giving of a sign; Christological problems (Son of the Most High, Davidic Kingship, Son of God), influence of Isaiah 7:10–14; Zechariah 9:9; Zephaniah 3:14–17; general problems of immaculate conception, so-called "virgin birth," and Mariology.)

III. Symbolic exploration questions

A. *Mothers, can you share something about the fears experienced during pregnancy?*

B. Mary was reflective and looking inward concerning all the experiences associated with her pregnancy. *Mothers, can you tell us something about Mary in you? Your private, inner thoughts and feelings while you were pregnant?*

C. Fathers, my own experience as a father tells me there was a lot going on with me during my wife's pregnancy. *How are you like Joseph? What were your anxieties, expectations, and thoughts about this new life?*

D. Mary was confronted with the mystery of something happening inside of her whose destiny she could not control, but had to accept passively. ("Here am I, the servant of the Lord; let it be with me according to your word"—Luke 1:38.) *Have you ever been confronted with a similar situation? How did you come to accept it as Mary did?*

E. Sometimes we say that there was a "pregnant" moment, meaning a time when something was getting ready to happen—preparing on the inside, and getting ready to happen in the near future. *How are you in a "pregnant" moment right now?*

IV. Conclusion

**Example #10. Symbolic Exploration Sermon
on the Birth Narratives**

Second Sermon:
Lessons of Giving Birth

Suggested Scripture: Luke 2:1–14

I. Guided meditation on Luke 2:1–7

II. Exposition
(Some reflections: Scholarly suggestions that Luke 2
can stand quite independently from Luke 1; Old Testament background in Psalm 87:6; Isaiah 1:3; Micah 4:5; 5:1;
problems with the term "betrothed" and the two-stage
process of Jewish marriage customs; dating problems with
the census; the cultural and symbolic significance of shepherds, particularly *Hermes*, conditions surrounding birth
in the ancient world, the annunciation pattern mentioned
in the last sermon, this time to the shepherds.)

III. Symbolic exploration questions

A. *Mothers, can you share with us just what the birth
experience feels like?*

B. *Fathers, what did you feel during the birth?*

C. Those of you who haven't experienced the birth of a
child yourself, I'm wondering if you, like the shepherds, have been given an announcement of something wonderful that's happened. *Imagine you are
the shepherd. How do you respond when someone
gives you a miraculous announcement? Are you
gullible? Are you skeptical?*

D. It is said that things are never the same after a
birth. That has certainly been true in my family.
But not just in the family situation, but inside

ourselves as well. *How did your perspective on life change after confronting a newborn baby? What did you see differently about yourself and about life?*

E. I want you to imagine now that you are holding a baby, just born, in your arms. Can you do that? A new baby. *What do you want to tell that child? What is the most important thing you want to say about the nature of life?*

IV. Conclusion

Parabling

"With many such parables he spoke the word to them, as they were able to hear it; he did not speak to them except in parables..." (Mark 4:33–34a).

Jesus' parables come from the most authentic level of the tradition. They confront us with an attitude that thinks symbolically, highlights opposites, and emphasizes reversals. The "how" of Jesus' parabling we do not know. From my own experience, I think we can hypothesize at the very least that, for us, parables emerge from the unconscious. For instance, a dream often portrays a life situation or an attitude through an image that we would not formerly have understood in that context. It might picture worship as a picnic, for example. As the images of worship and picnic collide, new meanings are generated for both. Depending upon our individual associations, we might find that we take worship too lightly (one association with "picnic"), or that a picnic may in fact be a sacred meal. I once dreamed, in a situation where I was thinking about leaving a congregation, that I was called to the boiler room of the church because there was no heat. When I inspected the boiler, I found that a tube carrying the hot water out to the system from the back of the boiler was completely riddled with holes, so that no water would flow. I took the tube out, repaired it as best I could, put it back, and the water began to flow a little bit. Not perfectly, but enough to give a little heat. That was the dream. Upon reflection I found it meaningful to understand my ministry at that congregation as a partially successful attempt to get the water flowing again and to give a little heat. Having done what I could, it was time to let a better plumber make the attempt.

Thus, the wisdom that Jesus' parables may have emerged from the unconscious invites us to wonder how we also might act upon the gifts given from our own unconscious in healing ways, and how we can follow through on unconscious images of conscious situations to revise our own standpoints and enliven our congregations. Notice that I have avoided saying that we "use" these images for a purpose. My understanding of the gifts of the unconscious is that they are not given for utilitarian purposes. They are not tools—just as the parables of Jesus are not utilitarian, not tricks of his trade. The healing is not in what we do to these images but in what they do to us! However, from time to time, it seems clear to me that, whatever the process that underlies the creation of a parabolic collision of images, we can embody those insights in sermons. I call that sermon style, *parabling*.

There is extensive literature in New Testament studies on the parables of Jesus. My distinction between primary and secondary language and my concern for rediscovering the "language-event" nature of the sermon comes from that tradition. Without reviewing that literature, let me begin this exploration of parabling with an insight into the nature of the parable:

> The crucial point is that a parable is metaphorical at every level and in every way—in language, in belief, in life. To say that it is metaphorical in language is obvious....The kingdom is never defined [in concepts]; it is spoken of in metaphorical language. But there is a deeper sense in which the parables are metaphoric. A parable is an *extended* metaphor—the metaphor is not in discrete images which allow for a flash of insight (a purely aesthetic or intellectual "Aha!"), but it is a way of believing and living that initially seems ordinary, yet it is so dislocated and rent from its usual context that, if the parable "works," spectators become participants....The secure, familiar everydayness of their own lives has been torn apart; they have seen another story...and they begin to understand (not just with their heads) that another way of believing and living—another context or frame for their lives—might be a possibility *for them*.[4]

[4]Sallie McFague, *Speaking in Parables: A Study in Metaphor and Theology*. Fortress Press, 1975, p. 78f.

I suggest that those words also describe an experience that can happen in parabling. A parabolic sermon aims at luring the spectators to become participants in order that "they begin to understand (not just with their heads) that another way of believing and living—another frame or context for their lives—might be a possibility *for them*."

Just how does a parabolic sermon "work"? As McFague suggests, the real work of a parable is the creation of a situation in which something that initially seems ordinary is unexpectedly placed in a new context or frame. For instance, Jesus starts talking about the common danger of robbers along the road from Jerusalem to Jericho, or a woman who lost a coin, or a man given stewardship of a sum of money. All of these are, at one level, familiar situations. But they are set in a most unusual context: "The kingdom of God is like...."

In the same way, a parabolic sermon seeks to talk about something that cannot be spoken, perhaps cannot be known, and is probably not in the conscious awareness of most people. That is the unusual context. There are many such issues in the life of any congregation: an important death, a change of leadership, prejudiced attitudes, pastor-parish conflict, a sense of despair concerning church decline. The list goes on. Denial is a powerful force in human life. And human beings in groups have ways of censoring anyone who would break the group silence around a particularly painful, conflictive, or angry topic. My conviction is that of course those things that are the most difficult to talk about are those things that most need to be worked through. Another entire arena of things that cannot be talked about in church has to do with things too deep for words: the meaning of the eucharist, the mysterious "glue" that binds a congregation together as a community, the "health" of the congregation, the momentum toward the future. Yet often a congregation needs to define precisely those kinds of things. But how do we talk about them from the heart rather than from the head? Finally, it is always difficult to comprehend and bring to language the unconscious currents that flow through the life of any congregation. We sense their reality, but rarely get a picture of the whole.

What cannot be talked about directly, for whatever reason, can be approached metaphorically. A parabolic sermon aims at creating a metaphor for talking about the unspeakable. It "preaches beside" an issue or a set of feelings, so to speak. A church is experiencing anxiety about something about to happen in the near future, so we preach about pregnancy. A church is facing a most important decison with long-lasting consequences, so we preach about Jesus in the Garden of Gethsemane. A church is still in pain over an experience in the past, so we preach on burying the dead. That is what I mean by "preaching beside": a sort of *doppel-gänger* in which a sermon about one thing is also somehow a sermon about something else and the congruency between the two experiences (the "metaphoric shock") is the impact of the sermon. I think we preach this way more than we realize, for to the discerning ear the stories we highlight in sermons usually have a great deal to do with our own life story. I want to suggest that parabling can be a way of speaking on different levels at the same time, which is intentional and conscious, as well as directed toward the needs of others rather than toward our own inner dilemmas.

For instance, let's take my dream of the broken boiler in the basement as a metaphor of the unconscious situation of the congregation. The metaphor of the boiler includes several aspects. The boiler provides heat to the building. In psychological terms, a failed boiler might suggest a "cold" church, lacking in emotional energy, feeling, and passion, especially spiritual energy. Also, the boiler powers a complicated system of pipes and pumps that flow through the building, providing it with warmth. In this case, I would lean toward the flowing water as a spiritual metaphor, suggesting that the spiritual source, sustenance, that should flow from the underground source has somehow dried up. The boiler image is not unrelated to the image of the vine and the branches in John 15, where the vine, also through a complicated system of "pipes," provides the branches with the sap that brings life and fruit. The dream pictures the problem not as a lack of fire (the boiler seems to work) but as a lack of a proper connection to the entire system (the pipe with holes).

So the dream image offers us the metaphor of a boiler to talk about the broken spiritual and emotional connection between the congregation and its source. It seems important to discover just how that plays out in the life of the congregation.

A traditional sermon might exhort folks to overcome the spiritual deadness, or simply describe the symptomatic conditions. But using a parabolic sermon, we invite people to experience the condition as a part of the sermon and already to begin to see it in a new light.

Using the parallel with the vine and branches, we might preach an interactive sermon on John 15. At the end of the exposition, we might offer the metaphor of the boiler as an illustration of the parable. Then, following up on the boiler image, we ask two symbolic exploration questions: (1) *Can you sense a time in your life in which it felt like somehow the water wasn't flowing from your inner boiler or power source?* (2) *What did you do to get your spiritual water flowing again?*

At this point we have a sermon about personal spirituality, which is probably quite helpful in and of itself. By asking those questions and hearing the response, most people in the congregation will be in touch with their own feelings, past and present, of emptiness, dryness, spiritual thirst. Very much as, in listening to the story of the good Samaritan, Jesus' listeners felt their own compassion stirred, so we now shift the frame for those feelings to the life context. Jesus' listeners thought they were hearing a story in which those in need are our neighbors (which is true, but fairly obvious to the ever ethical Pharisees), but he parabolically shifts the frame—"Who proved neighbor to the man who fell among the robbers?—so that those compassionate feelings are suddenly directed toward the Samaritan enemy (an unexpected ethic of care for the neighbor)—a different context. We ask the third question,

(3) *Can you sense a time when it felt to you like the water wasn't flowing from our spiritual source (inner boiler / power source) as a church?* And suddenly we're talking about the context of a church experience and hadn't ever really been conscious of just how dry, empty, thirsty, we had actually felt in church before.

After wrestling with those feelings for a while, the fourth and concluding question might be simply: (4) *What do you need to do to get the water flowing?*

That example illustrates the two most important aspects of parabling. A parabolic sermon creates a metaphor that "talks beside" the feelings or thoughts we want to be shared. The metaphor provides the symbolic kind of experience we can talk about. Secondly, having gained access to those inner feelings or thoughts, we then shift to a life context, and all of a sudden we are at a moment of discovery and revelation. So a parabolic sermon might be understood as *a sermon that enters the inner experience through the symbolic level and then shifts the frame to the life context level.*

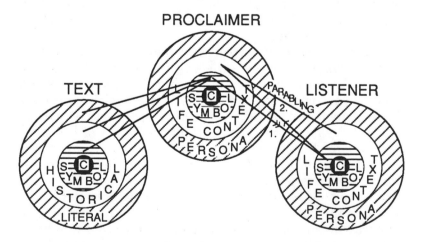

Ideally, we begin to understand those original feelings or ideas in a new way as a result of the "reframing."

Reframing is a second important concept in parabling. It comes from the strategic or paradoxical school of family therapy. As we discussed in chapter two, the technique is used to give old behavior new meaning. It offers new ways of understanding and interpreting old situations.

Parabling is reframing. In these sermons we explicitly invite people to talk about symbolic experiences, or to understand their own experience in deeper ways. The third question in the example above—*Can you sense a time when it felt to you like the water wasn't flowing from our spiritual source (inner boiler/power source) in this church?*—reframes those personal feelings of emptiness as church-related expressions as well. But the reframing, or a deeper perhaps second-level "meta"-reframing, lies in the initial metaphor. From the very beginning of that sermon, the image of the boiler or the vine and branches already gives us a new way of understanding our feelings of spiritual dryness. In the examples that follow, simply talking about the most difficult things we have ever had to do within the framework of Jesus' experience in Gethsemane gives a new perspective to those predicaments.

A parabolic sermon makes the reframing an intentional movement of the sermon. In parabling, we set out to elicit a set of attitudes, images, or feelings that closely relate metaphorically to the life context we want to talk about later. Initially we ask people to experience those attitudes, images, or feelings symbolically. In the following example we invite people to enter imaginatively into the disciples' attitudes in the feeding stories. Then we shift the frame, bringing those same attitudes, images, or feelings into a life context. For instance, the new frame for those attitudes suddenly becomes the context of our own attitudes about worship. The metaphoric link between the disciples' attitudes about the miracle and our attitudes about worship reframe our understanding about both sets of attitudes.

The process and form of a parabolic sermon might look something like this:

1. Conception

This occurs before the actual preaching of the sermon. The conception grows out of a perceived need, a dream image, a metaphor, a new vision of faith and meaning—whatever the mysterious process of the creation may be. For instance, let's use the dream image of worship as a picnic mentioned above.

2. Scriptural Parallels

The process of taking the initial conception of the parable and transforming it into a sermon involves a lot of imaginative work. First we have to understand the "field" created by the metaphor. For instance, worship as picnic suggests either that we take worship too lightly or that simple acts of daily life such as breaking bread together have sacred undertones. So the field is something about our attitude toward worship, which probably needs to be revised. Upon reflection we may see that worship in our particular congregation has become focused on personal experience and the formal aspects of worship, to the exclusion of a more communal experience and informal aspects (like a picnic). As we start to get a feel for the field, the metaphor suggests we can begin to open ourselves to scriptures that parallel the issue. While there are several possibilities, I find the gospel stories of the feeding of the multitude the best parallel. The metaphor already offers a new frame for understanding the pericope, for in fact, people are gathered there for a feeding that is not unlike a church picnic, although we might never have made that connection before. Mark 8:1ff. even suggests that the disciples are not understanding the sacredness of the meal seriously enough (verses 16–21). With that parallel we have the material for a sermon.

3. Introduction

Our sermon would begin with a solid exegesis of the text. Because the field of our metaphor has to do with our attitudes about worship, I would focus the exegesis on the disciples' response to the feeding, rather than on the miracle itself. Some exegetical points might concern the role of the disciples in the Gospel of Mark (they are consistently represented as misunderstanding Jesus' mission), the significance of the numbers 12 and 7, and Mark's "framing" of certain stories (our story is preceded by the healing of the deaf and dumb, and followed by the healing of a blind man).

4. The Metaphor

We now want to introduce the metaphor of worship as picnic. This is done with symbolic exploration questions. So I might say something like: "Have you ever noticed that this miracle on the grass is like a church picnic? etc." Then, using the frame of the miracle story, we ask people to participate in the metaphor. Since our field is attitudes, that's the way the questions should run: (1) *Imagine you are one of the disciples. What is it about your attitude toward the picnic that prevents you from understanding the meaning of the meal in the way Jesus did?* That question brings people into the story, but not personally. So the next question needs to ask them to speak from their own experience. (2) *Can you tell a story about a time when your disciple, your attitude toward what was proper or improper, kept you from joining in "the picnic" or joining in the fun?*

5. The Reframing

Now we want to switch the frame from attitudes about "the picnic" to life context of worship experiences. (3) *Are there times when your attitude toward what is proper or improper prevents you from joining in the spirit of worship here?*

6. Conclusion

The conclusion should simply tie together the themes that have run through the dialogue—in this case, something about how often our preset attitudes get in the way of our experiencing worship, or simply life as it happens. The gospel story seems to point to the power of Jesus to overcome the things that hold us back, to hear what we couldn't hear before, say what we couldn't say, and see what we couldn't see.

From such a general example, "worship as picnic," it is difficult to see how such a metaphorical connection speaks to an authentic need. Yet if we imagine such a dream coming from a church in a quite rigid situation, then the impact of the metaphor and sermon is clear. I believe this demonstrates something about parables that biblical scholarship has also noticed. Parables arise in unique and particular frames, and are thus intrinsically wed to the moment they are spoken. Change the frame of the parable and the interpretation changes. This is as true of a parabolic sermon as it is of the parables of Jesus. I want to stress that, from their conception, parabolic sermons must speak to particular situations in particular moments of the life of particular congregations. These sermons seek to enter and transform unique situations that exist only in a given moment of time. Like Jesus' parables, they are not preached for cleverness or fun, but to open new ways of being that are called for at the time.

Parabling is difficult. It requires a symbolic, metaphorical way of understanding the life around us. I hope from the examples and form given above that some understanding is emerging of the parabling process toward which I am aiming. Even with so extended a section as this, there remains much to be said about parabling. For instance, a sermon does not need to be interactive to be parabolic, although I have found that the interaction is essential in drawing the listeners into the story. Also, there are clearly other forms a parabolic sermon could take, as well as other ways of understanding the meaning and uses of parables. A great deal more needs to be said about the psychology of the parable, and the connections between sermons and paradoxical psychotherapy offer rich implications. Probably, parabolic sermons can be manipulative and dangerous, raising serious ethical questions. But all of these issues aside, I find that parabling can be a powerful and healing preaching technique that invites people to experience their own attitudes and feelings in new and enriching ways.

Example #11. Parabolic Sermon:

In His Footsteps

Suggested Scripture: Matthew 26:36–44

I. Conception

A. The situation: The congregation is faced with a decision about whether to renovate the old building or relocate to a new building. There are a lot of difficult feelings about even the suggestion that a move might be necessary, but no one seems to be able to talk about that.

B. After a meeting on the subject, a man suggests to me, "This will be the hardest thing this congregation has ever had to do."

II. Scriptural parallel
The idea of "the hardest thing this congregation has ever had to do" led me quickly to thinking about the hardest things that people have to do over the course of a lifetime. That connection is a metaphor for beginning to see how an institution faces a difficult decision. Thus the field of the metaphor is really a set of attitudes, or stories that reveal attitudes, about how one best should face difficult situations. I felt sure there were some important stories behind that question. And that led to scriptural stories where someone had to do something that was obviously difficult for them, and by far the best parallel was the story of Jesus in Gethsemane.

III. Introduction

A. Guided meditation on Matthew 26:36–44, in the present tense and asking people to notice the details of the scene in visual, auditory, and kinesthetic terms.

    B. After leading the meditation, ask people to report what they saw, heard, and felt there in Gethsemane.

    C. Brief remarks about the uniqueness of the story showing Jesus' hesitation, Old Testament parallels to the garden scene, the importance of this story in tying together the Last Supper which precedes it and the arrest that follows it.

IV. The metaphor

    A. Symbolic exploration question: In thinking about just how difficult a moment this was in Jesus' life, I want to ask you an important question. We all follow in Jesus footsteps, so let me ask, *When have you entered the garden of Gethsemane? What do you feel is the most difficult thing you have ever had to do in your life (or one of the most difficult)?*

    B. Symbolic exploration question: *What was the answer to your prayer that if it be possible, you might not have to drink from that cup?*

V. The reframing
Directed question: *What feelings surface when you touch the most difficult thing our congregation faces?*

VI. Conclusion
Symbolic exploration question: *What would your inner Jesus say about facing the most difficult things?*

Example #12. Parabolic Sermon:

Burying the Dead

Suggested Scripture: Luke 9:52—10:2

I. Conception

People in the congregation are telling stories about the time when several families left the church over some forgotten controversy. As a result, the congregation is avoiding conflict at all cost. The guiding perception of people about the state of the church is one of loss and depression. One of those former members dies, and all those old stories surface and the feelings come to a head. The metaphor is the parallel between the way we work through grief in our own life and the way a church should work through grief. The common field between personal loss and church losses is the feeling experience of loss.

II. Scriptural parallels

There are a lot of stories about people dealing with loss in the scriptures. I particularly like John 16:19–24, where Jesus could be said to reframe the disciples' grief over his impending death as the pain of a woman in birth. It gives suffering an entirely different connotation. But for this sermon, I could not escape the clear parallels in Luke 9 where people are insisting on taking care of old business when Jesus is saying there is a mission.

III. Introduction

A. Guided meditation on Luke 9:52—10:2.

B. Exegetical considerations—the emphasis on the cost of discipleship in Luke.

IV. The metaphor

A. Symbolic exploration question: *Imagine you are the one who has been called by Jesus, but ask first to have time for your grief. What are you feeling?*

B. Symbolic exploration question: *When did you finally let go? What has to happen before you feel
ready to let go?*

V. The reframing

Directed question: *Can you remember a time when you
felt important losses here at church?*

VI. Conclusion

A. Psychological distinction between grief and depression: Grief is the natural slowing down of the
entire body during which time a person's view of
self in the world is restructured. Depression can be
understood as the lack of the ability to restructure
our view of ourselves in the world.

B. Symbolic exploration question: Jesus said, "Let the
dead bury their own dead; but as for you, go and
proclaim the kingdom of God" (Luke 9:60). *How
have you been trying to hold on, and not letting go
like the man in the parable?*

C. Directed Question: *What vision of the future comes
to mind when you look to the future of our church?*

CONCLUSION

These four models represent just some of the possibilities with interactive preaching. I have suggested specific ways of aiming for a deeper engagement of the life context and symbolic levels in the listener. This requires that we as proclaimers must also engage the deeper levels in ourselves and especially in the texts. I also want to reemphasize that these levels are not so clear cut as I have described them. In reality, these levels interpenetrate our awareness all the time, speaking unpredictably from moment to moment. Furthermore, I would never venture to say just in what measure the core is touched. That is the mystery. We never know to what extent the greater self in us, the living God, lives and moves and has being, claiming us for something larger than our human willing.

I do speak with the conviction that such a revelation of the core is experiential, and in the end indescribable. That is what Paul Riceour calls the "radical incommunicability of human experience as lived." My conviction is that our sermons never *communicate* that experience, for human experience remains a mystery. Try as we may, we cannot give our experience to another, even to those whom we love. Our descriptions, however authentic, however grand, can never substitute for what another must truly live in order truly to know.

Therefore, I have offered interactive preaching as a model not so much to communicate the experience but rather as an attempt at relational experience. What we offer in a sermon is ourselves, an "I" who seeks a "Thou." What we offer is a relationship, our own person in a subjective life context and pattern in which the symbols

151

move. What matters is not so much what we say as who we are in the very midst of relationship. That is the true sermon.

Yet the mystery, the particularly Christian mystery perhaps, is that in this "I" who we are and those "Thous" to whom we offer ourselves as proclaimers is incarnated the living God, so that, in relating, when we offer ourselves we offer God, and in receiving we receive God. That is the mystery.